# DEDICATION

To three integrated learners I know:

The poet, who navigates the stars;

The drummer, who touches others' souls;

and

The inventor, who notes nature's ways.

# THE MINDFUL SCHOOL

# HOW TO INTEGRATE THE CURRICULA

by

Robin Fogarty

Skylight Publishing, Inc.
Palatine, Illinois

## Other Books By the Same Author

- Designs for Cooperative Interactions
  *12 strategies to help you move toward more interactive teaching models with your students*

- Blueprints for Thinking in the Cooperative Classroom
  *Combines the most effective techniques for stimulating higher-order thinking with a synthesis of the best practices in cooperative learning*

- Patterns for Thinking
  *An innovative staff development program that offers a spectrum of practical strategies to help teachers integrate curricula and assist with transfer*

- Start Them Thinking
  *Provides the K-3 teacher with practical strategies and lesson plans for introducing young students to the fun and rigors of skillful thinking*

- Catch Them Thinking
  *A handbook of strategies for teaching thinking*

- Teach Them Thinking
  *An inventory of 24 essential thinking skills*

- Keep Them Thinking II
  *Highly-detailed step-by-step model lessons that show you exactly what to do to implement thinking in your classroom*

**The Mindful School: How To Integrate the Curricula**
First Printing

Published by Skylight Publishing, Inc.
200 East Wood Street, Suite 250
Palatine, Illinois 60067
800-922-4474 (in Illinois 708-991-6300)
FAX 708-991-6420

Editing: Julia E. Noblitt
Book Design: Bruce Leckie
Illustration: David Stockman
Type Composition: Donna Ramirez
Production Coordination: Ari Ohlson

Library of Congress Catalog Card Number: 91-60963

ISBN #0-932935-31-1

# ► CONTENTS ◄

# FOREWORD

The mindful classroom is composed of engaged students, the teacher being one of them. Robin Fogarty's *How To Integrate the Curricula* gives the teacher the opportunity to be a learner. Her exercises and images provoke new perspectives on the curriculum. They also give young people a handle on the concept of interdisciplinary thinking.

In these pages, readers will find practical suggestions supported by strong theoretical underpinnings. Fogarty prompts active reflection on our own work settings and curriculum development projects. Teachers and staff developers will find this book a useful tool for inservice workshops and personal reading. The hope is to encourage all learners in the classroom to be thoughtful, creative, and, mindful.

Heidi Hayes Jacobs
Columbia University Teachers College
New York City
March, 1991

# ACKNOWLEDGMENTS

I remember reading once in someone's introduction that, "This book took a year—plus a lifetime to write!" The thoughts shared here represent an accumulation of ideas over time and present the core of the integrated learner model. Learners must constantly and continually make connections. As they proceed on their journeys, they single-mindedly dig into an idea and at the same time they network with others for breadth across related fields. As a result, concepts come into focus and emerge as beliefs that propel the learner even further along in his or her chosen path and into never-ending circles of expert associates. In my work with curriculum and cognitive instruction, there are two external camps of "expert" associates that have influenced my thinking about how to integrate the curricula: the expert *theorists* and the expert *practitioners.*

In the theorists camp, I'd like to acknowledge Heidi Hayes Jacobs for providing the initial impetus for this work. Her chapter, "Design Options for an Integrated Curriculum" *(Interdisciplinary Curriculum*, ASCD, 1989), acted as a catalyst for the ideas presented in this book.

In addition, I'm especially grateful to David Perkins for his illuminating article on finding fertile themes with which to integrate curricula. With his rich criteria, this thematic model takes on new integrity. In the absence of applied criteria, topical themes are often superficial, with content artificially included or excluded accordingly. David's "lenses" provide the needed rigor. In addition, thanks go to David for the idea of the characters placed in a school setting. This sparked the inclusion of the comics that appear throughout the book.

Finally, also in the theorists camp, I'd like to thank Art Costa for his initial review of the integrated models and his timely suggestion for one that illustrates how a teacher targets several ideas in a single lesson or nests several ideas together—thus, the "nested" model that appears as Integrated Model #3.

Now, in the practitioner's camp, there are three distinct expert *flanks*: teachers from Carpentersville, Illinois; teachers from the Waterford Schools in Pontiac, Michigan; and teachers from the Richmond School District in Richmond, British Columbia, Canada.

Last summer, elementary and middle school teachers from Carpentersville, Illinois, worked on models to help integrate the curricula for lessons and learners. Some of their actual lesson designs appear as examples in the book. My thanks for their early efforts with me in exploring this idea of an integrated curriculum: Carol Bonebrake, Jane Atherton, Suzanne Raymond, Barbara Bengston, Al Eck, Kathleen Vehring, Roseanne Day, Nancy Blackman, Clifford Berutti, Linda Morning, Diane Gray, and Terri Pellant.

My thanks to Julie Casteel and her teachers in Michigan, especially Al Monetta, Chris Brakke, Lori Broughton, and Sue Barber who provided the topics to fill in the first model on page 8 of this book. At IRI/Skylight Publishing, Inc., we know that if Julie is doing it, it must be the next educational innovation. A pioneer practitioner leading the thinking skills movement into action research teams, she is once again on the cutting edge with the integrated learning idea. My thanks to both Julie and her "risk-taking" staff for letting me test the models with real teachers.

My sincere thanks to my friends and colleagues in Canada. First to Carol-Lyn Sakata who brought me there, then to Bruce Beairsto, David Shore, and Darlene Macklam, for introducing me to the teachers of Richmond. Their heroic efforts to implement a visionary provincial document, "Year 2000: A Framework for Learning" has continued to inspire my work. I am especially indebted to one teacher, Heather MacLaren. Last spring, she asked her seventh graders to prepare to talk at their parent conferences about what they had done that year and how all the things they had learned overlapped and were connected. The students' intricate Venn diagrams provided graphic representations of integrating the curricula as perceived through the eyes of the learners. These drawings sparked my own thinking about creative, integrative models.

In addition, working with eighty teachers in a summer workshop in Richmond called "Teaching For Transfer," John Barell, David Perkins, and I (with the help of "Captain Transfer," our superhero), had a first stab at trying to help teachers sift out curricular priorities. This, too, served as an initial springboard for my ideas about how to integrate the curricula. Also, special thanks to Monica Pamer, Gina Rae, and Jacquie Anderson for their conversations and encouragement.

Finally, I would be remiss if I neglected to mention my internal network of colleagues. My thanks to: Jim Bellanca for his faith in me and my ideas; Bruce Leckie for the *design* part that not only shaped, but propelled the *writing* part; David Stockman for his cover art and comic art; Julie Noblitt for her editor's eye; Donna Ramirez for her ability to decipher my handwriting; and to Ari Ohlson for getting this book off our desks and off to press!

# INTRODUCTION

*To the young mind every thing is individual, stands by itself. By and by, it finds how to join two things and see in them one nature; then three, then three thousand; and so, tyrannized over by its own unifying instinct, it goes on tying things together, diminishing anomalies, discovering roots running underground whereby contrary and remote things cohere and flower out from one stem... The astronomer discovers that geometry, a pure abstraction of the human mind, is the measure of planetary motion. The chemist finds proportions and intelligible method throughout matter; and science is nothing but the finding of analogy, identity, in the most remote parts.—Emerson*

## What Is This Book All About?

To help the "young mind...[discover] roots running under ground whereby contrary and remote things cohere and flower out from one stem" is at once the mission of the teacher and of the learner. To that end, this first book in The Mindful School series presents models to connect and integrate the curricula.

What does "integrating the curricula" mean? Does it mean sifting out the parcels of each overloaded discipline and focusing on the priorities in depth? . . . (Fragmented)

Does it mean integrating or connecting yesterday's lesson to today's topic? Or relating all issues studied in the science class to the concept of evolution in biology? Or does it mean integrating threads such as "power" and "isolation" woven throughout the Social Studies topics? . . . (Connected)

Does it mean targeting multidimensional skills and concepts within one lesson? . . . . (Nested)

Does it mean rearranging the sequence of when a topic is taught to coincide with a parallel topic in another content? . . . (Sequenced)

Does it mean integrating one subject with another through the learner's conceptual eye? . . . (Shared)

Does it mean selecting an overall theme (such as "persistence" or "argument," or a topic as familiar as "transportation") and using a thematic umbrella across all disciplines? Or selecting a book or era or artist and weaving the fabric of the disciplines into that selected context? . . . (Webbed)

Does it mean integrating the content of what is taught with cognitive tools and cooperative strategies that cross disciplines and spill into life situations? . . . (Threaded)

Does integrating the curricula encompass interdisciplinary team planning in which conceptual overlaps become the common focus across departments? . . . (Integrated)

Does it mean integrative threads within the learner himself/herself that connect past experiences and prior knowledge with new information and novel experiences? . . . (Immersed)

Does it mean reaching out to build bonds with other experts through networking? . . . (Networked)

The answer, of course, is that integrating the curricula can be any or all (and more) of the aforementioned models. Each teacher and each learner views the integration process differently. Yet, there is a common vision encompassing three distinct dimensions that is commonly accepted.

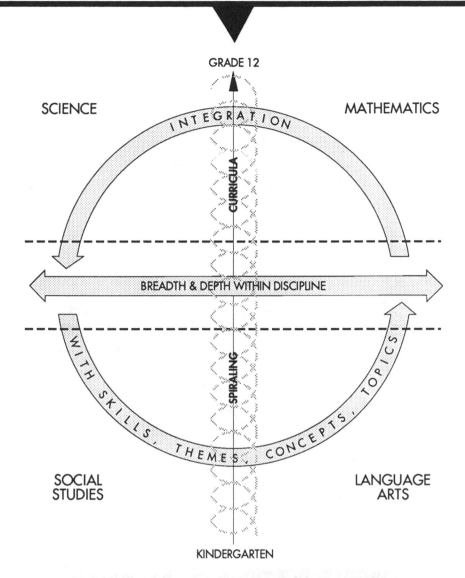

**HOW TO INTEGRATE CURRICULA: THREE DIMENSIONS**

The vertical spiral represents the "spiraling" curricula built into most text materials as content is integrated and revisited through the K-12 grades. Mastery of certain material is expected at each level in preparation for "building on to that for the next concepts," at subsequent levels. Integration occurs vertically throughout the schooling years.

The horizontal band represents the breadth and depth of learning in a given subject. As different subjects are approached, explored, and learned *within* each discipline, a cumulative effect is anticipated. Students are to expand their conceptual bases for future learning in related fields: one math concept builds toward the next as ideas are integrated within a discipline.

Finally, the circle represents the integration of skills, themes, concepts, and topics *across* disciplines as similarities are noted. These explicit connections are used to enhance the learning in a wholistic manner as students link ideas from one subject to ideas in another subject.

In summary, both integration *within* a discipline and integration *across* disciplines are necessary to fully integrate the curricula.

To further explore this idea, this book will present detailed discussions on a range of models. Beginning with an exploration *within single disciplines*, at the left end of the spectrum, and continuing with models that integrate *across several disciplines*, the continuum ends with models that integrate *within* the learner himself and finally *across* networks of other learners.

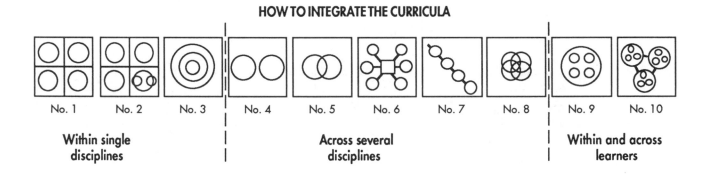

HOW TO INTEGRATE THE CURRICULA

| No. 1 | No. 2 | No. 3 | No. 4 | No. 5 | No. 6 | No. 7 | No. 8 | No. 9 | No. 10 |

Within single disciplines | Across several disciplines | Within and across learners

This book presents ten models that represent ten different views for integrating the curricula. (See chart on opposite page.)

## How Do Teachers Use the Book?

The book is divided into ten sections, one for each of the models. The discussion for each model includes answers to the following questions:

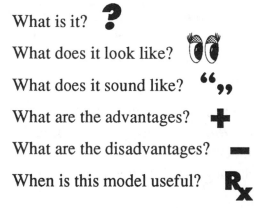

What is it? **?**

What does it look like?

What does it sound like? **" ,,**

What are the advantages? **+**

What are the disadvantages? **—**

When is this model useful? **Rx**

To complete the discussion of each model, a vignette of teachers working with the model is presented in comic-book style. The scenarios depict the ongoing interaction of four faculty members trying to integrate the curricula.

# Toward an Integrated Curriculum

### Ten Views for Integrating the Curricula: How Do You See It?

**1**

**Fragmented**

Periscope—one direction; one sighting; narrow focus on single discipline

**Description**
The traditional model of separate and distinct disciplines, which fragments the subject areas.

**Example**
Teacher applies this view in Math, Science, Social Studies, Language Arts OR Sciences, Humanities, Fine and Practical Arts.

**2**

**Connected**

Opera glass—details of one discipline; focus on subtleties and interconnections

**Description**
Within each subject area, course content is connected topic to topic, concept to concept, one year's work to the next, and relates idea(s) explicitly.

**Example**
Teacher relates the concept of fractions to decimals, which in turn relates to money, grades, etc.

**3**

**Nested**

3-D glasses—multiple dimensions to one scene, topic, or unit

**Description**
Within each subject area, the teacher targets multiple skills: a social skill, a thinking skill, and a content-specific skill.

**Example**
Teacher designs the unit on photosynthesis to simultaneously target consensus seeking (social skill), sequencing (thinking skill), and plant life cycle (science content).

**4**

**Sequenced**

Eyeglasses—varied internal content framed by broad, related concepts

**Description**
Topics or units of study are rearranged and sequenced to coincide with one another. Similar ideas are taught in concert while remaining separate subjects.

**Example**
English teacher presents an historical novel depicting a particular period while the History teacher teaches that same historical period.

**5**

**Shared**

Binoculars—two disciplines that share overlapping concepts and skills

**Description**
Shared planning and teaching take place in two disciplines in which overlapping concepts or ideas emerge as organizing elements.

**Example**
Science and Math teachers use data collection, charting, and graphing as shared concepts that can be team-taught.

**6**

**Webbed**

Telescope—broad view of an entire constellation as one theme, webbed to the various elements

**Description**
A fertile theme is webbed to curriculum contents and disciplines; subjects use the theme to sift out appropriate concepts, topics, and ideas.

**Example**
Teacher presents a simple topical theme, such as the circus, and webs it to the subject areas. A conceptual theme, such as conflict, can be webbed for more depth in the theme approach.

**7**

**Threaded**

Magnifying glass—big ideas that magnify all content through a metacurricular approach

**Description**
The metacurricular approach threads thinking skills, social skills, multiple intelligences, technology, and study skills through the various disciplines.

**Example**
Teaching staff targets prediction in Reading, Math, and Science lab experiments while Social Studies teacher targets forecasting current events, and thus threads the skill (prediction) across disciplines.

**8**

**Integrated**

Kaleidoscope—new patterns and designs that use the basic elements of each discipline

**Description**
This interdisciplinary approach matches subjects for overlaps in topics and concepts with some team teaching in an authentic integrated model.

**Example**
In Math, Science, Social Studies, Fine Arts, Language Arts, and Practical Arts, teachers look for patterning models and approach content through these patterns.

**9**

**Immersed**

Microscope—intensely personal view that allows microscopic explanation as all content is filtered through lens of interest and expertise

**Description**
The disciplines become part of the learner's lens of expertise; the learner filters all content through this lens and becomes immersed in his or her own experience.

**Example**
Student or doctoral candidate has an area of expert interest and sees all learning through that lens.

**10**

**Networked**

Prism—a view that creates multiple dimensions and directions of focus

**Description**
Learner filters all learning through the expert's eye and makes internal connections that lead to external networks of experts in related fields.

**Example**
Architect, while adapting the CAD/CAM technology for design, networks with technical programmers and expands her knowledge base, just as she had traditionally done with interior designers.

© Robin Fogarty, 1991*

*Extrapolated from "Design Options for an Integrated Curriculum" by Heidi Hayes Jacobs in *Interdisciplinary Curriculum*, ASCD, 1989.

MARIA NOVELAS

SUE SUM

BOB BEAKER

THOMAS TIME

CAPT. META COGNITION

Maria Novelas, the Language Arts teacher, has been with the district for seventeen years, while Sue Sum is a recent graduate who landed a job in the Math department. Bob Beaker has manned his Science lab in The Mindful School for the past five years, but Thomas Time has been in the History department "since time began."

In addition to the four staff members, there is Priscilla Pauley, the progressive principal who supports her teachers in their effort to more fully integrate the curricula. Also, several graduates of The Mindful School round out the vignettes of the integrated learner models. Throughout the book, guiding comments are made by Captain Meta Cognition, our super-hero, who provides a freeze-frame, metacognitive comment about the various views of curricular integration.

 Following the comic-strip action, each section ends with a set of four pages of graphics. These organizers are included for reader use. The first graphic in each model provides an actual sample of curricular integration for teachers to study and discuss. The three subsequent graphics include directions for immediate reader use. One requires teachers to *look back* and *redesign* familiar lessons or units. Another graphic requires the teachers to *look ahead* and *design* lessons and units with upcoming material, while the final graphic simply suggests that teachers *look again* to *refine* and/or *redesign* lessons or units.

Whether you are working alone, with partners, or in teams, the organizers provide immediate and visible transfer of the models into useful prototypes. In fact, a faculty can easily work with this over time to develop integrated curricula throughout the school. Each staff member or team can choose one model to work with each semester. As teachers begin the conversation about integrating the curricula, the spectrum of models becomes more inviting. Or, students themselves can work with the models to explore the connections they make within and across disciplines and within and across learners.

## Now What?

The models presented are just beginnings. Teachers can use and reuse them as they conceptualize and reconceptualize "What's worth teaching?" and "How do I best present that to students?" In addition to these models teachers can invent their own designs for integrating the curricula. The process never ends. It's a cycle that offers renewed energy to each school year as teachers help "the young mind...[discover] roots running under ground whereby contrary and remote things cohere and flower out from one stem."

SOMETIMES IT'S GOOD TO GET
A SINGLE SIGHTING OF EACH
SUBJECT — LIKE LOOKING
THROUGH A PERISCOPE.

# Model

## FRAGMENTED

*The traditional model of separate and distinct disciplines, which fragments the subject areas.*

Periscope—one direction; one sighting; narrow focus on single discipline

*"Education is the instruction of the intellect in the laws of Nature."* —Thomas Huxley

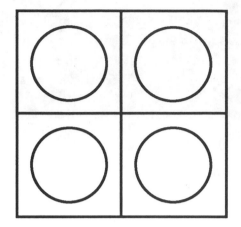

## What Is The Fragmented Model?

The traditional curricular arrangement dictates separate and distinct disciplines. Typically, the four major academic areas are labeled Math, Science, Language Arts, and Social Studies. Fine Arts and Practical Arts pick up the remaining subjects of Art, Music, and Physical Education which are often considered "soft subjects" when compared to the "hard-core" academic areas. Another grouping of the disciplines uses the categories of Humanities, Sciences, Practical Arts, and Fine Arts. In the standard curriculum, these subject matter areas are taught in isolation, with no attempt to connect or integrate them. Each is seen as a pure entity in and of itself. While there may well be overlaps in the sciences of physics and chemistry, the relationships between the two are implicitly, not explicitly, approached through the curriculum.

EXAMPLE:

**Teacher applies this view in Math, Science, Social Studies, Language Arts OR Sciences, Humanities, Fine and Practical Arts.**

## What Does It Look Like?

In the secondary school or junior high, each discipline is taught by different teachers in different locations throughout the building with the students moving to different rooms. Each separate encounter carries with it a separate and distinct cellular organization leaving the student with a fragmented view of the curricula. A less severe model of fragmentation, with subjects still taught separately and apart from each other, is the elementary classroom. In this situation the teacher says, "Now, put away your

Math books and take out your Science packets. It's time to work on our Science unit." The daily schedule shows distinct time slots for Math, Science, or Social Studies. Rarely are topics from two areas intentionally correlated. This isolation of subjects is still the norm, even in the self-contained classroom.

## What Does It Sound Like?

A young high school student explained the fragmented curriculum like a vaccination: "Math is not Science, Science is not English, English is not History. A subject is something you take once and need never take again. It's like getting a vaccination; I've had my shot of algebra. I'm done with that."

In one day, a typical junior-high school student may be asked to perform in seven or eight very different subjects, from mathematics to P. E. The student will do this every day in addition to the homework each subject will generate. In order to cope with such a work load, students may have to choose between focusing on the one or two subjects they enjoy doing and excel in them, and doing the minimum required to "get by" in each subject. We may wonder, "What do students learn under these circumstances?" and "Are the needs of the system taking precedence over the needs of the students?"

## What Are The Advantages?

One of the advantages of this fragmented model, of course, is that the purity of each discipline is left untainted. In addition, instructors prepare as experts in a field and have the luxury of digging into their subject with both breadth and depth. This traditional model also provides a comfort zone for all concerned because it represents the norm. We're used to it. The weight of these pluses must not be taken too lightly. There is value in examining one discipline or subject as a separate and distinct entity in order to reveal the critical attributes of each discrete field. This model, although fragmented, does provide clear and discrete views of the disciplines. Experts can easily sift out the priorities of their own subject areas. Also, students realize the benefits of working with a mentor in this model.

> STUDENTS, PARENTS, AND TEACHERS—THEY'RE WONDERING HOW IT ALL FITS.

## What Are The Disadvantages?

The disadvantages are twofold. The learner is left to his own resources to make connections or integrate similar concepts. In addition, overlapping concepts, skills, and attitudes are not illuminated for the learner and transfer of learning to novel situations is less likely to occur. To leave the learner unattended in making connections both within and across the disciplines is to overlook some of the latest research on transfer of learning which calls for explicit bridging. Also, in this discipline-based model, students can easily get caught in the avalanche of work. Although each teacher assigns a reasonable amount, the cumulative effect can become overwhelming for the students.

## When Is This Fragmented Model Useful?

This is a useful curricular configuration for large schools with diverse populations in which a variety of course offerings that provide a spectrum of subjects can target special interests. It's most useful at the university level where students travel on specialized paths of study that require expert knowledge for instructing, mentoring, coaching, and collaborating. Prior to the university level, this model is helpful to the teacher, whose preparation can be more focused. It is also a good model for teachers who want to sift out curricular priorities before using cross-departmental models for interdisciplinary planning.

LET'S NOT DISMISS THE TRADITIONAL MODEL TOO LIGHTLY. IT'S WORKED FOR MANY YEARS. THERE MUST BE A REASON IT HAS SURVIVED THE TEST OF TIME.

I'LL HAVE THEM WATCH THE TV VERSION OF MACBETH AS WEEKEND HOMEWORK. THEN STUDENTS WILL BE FAMILIAR WITH THE PLOT, AND THEY CAN CONCENTRATE ON THE BEAUTY OF SHAKESPEAREAN ENGLISH.

MEANWHILE, BACK AT THE MINDFUL SCHOOL, TEACHERS WITH PERISCOPIC VISION ARE UNINTENTIONALLY BURYING THEIR STUDENTS WITH HOMEWORK... AS MARIA NOVELAS, THOMAS TIME, SUE SUM, AND BOB BEAKER INDIVIDUALLY PLAN THEIR CURRICULA...

THIS LIST OF TOPICS WILL HELP STUDENTS SELECT THEIR SEMESTER PROJECTS ON WESTERN CIVILIZATION. I WANT THEM TO USE THE WEEKEND TO BEGIN THEIR SEARCH.

IF I GET THEM STARTED IN CLASS TODAY, THE STUDENTS SHOULD BE ABLE TO GET A GOOD START ON THESE THEOREMS OVER THE WEEKEND.

I WILL ASSIGN THE CHAPTER READING OVER THE WEEKEND TO INTRODUCE THE PERIODIC TABLE OF ELEMENTS. THAT WAY THEY WILL HAVE TIME TO REALLY DIG IN AND LEARN IT FOR USE THIS SEMESTER.

*In each discipline, six priority units or topics are listed. They are ranked according to importance to overall curricular requirements.*

# ► Samples ◄

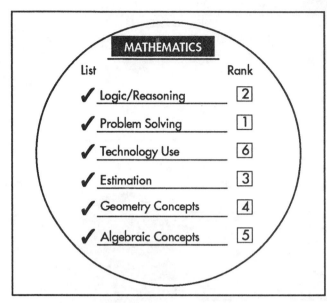

**MATHEMATICS**

| List | Rank |
|------|------|
| ✓ Logic/Reasoning | 2 |
| ✓ Problem Solving | 1 |
| ✓ Technology Use | 6 |
| ✓ Estimation | 3 |
| ✓ Geometry Concepts | 4 |
| ✓ Algebraic Concepts | 5 |

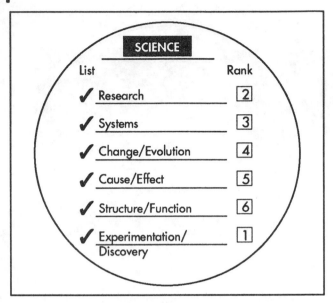

**SCIENCE**

| List | Rank |
|------|------|
| ✓ Research | 2 |
| ✓ Systems | 3 |
| ✓ Change/Evolution | 4 |
| ✓ Cause/Effect | 5 |
| ✓ Structure/Function | 6 |
| ✓ Experimentation/Discovery | 1 |

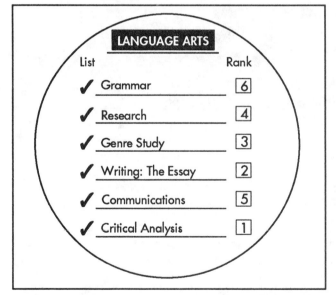

**LANGUAGE ARTS**

| List | Rank |
|------|------|
| ✓ Grammar | 6 |
| ✓ Research | 4 |
| ✓ Genre Study | 3 |
| ✓ Writing: The Essay | 2 |
| ✓ Communications | 5 |
| ✓ Critical Analysis | 1 |

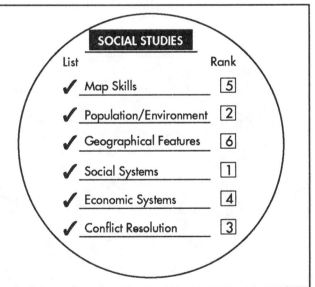

**SOCIAL STUDIES**

| List | Rank |
|------|------|
| ✓ Map Skills | 5 |
| ✓ Population/Environment | 2 |
| ✓ Geographical Features | 6 |
| ✓ Social Systems | 1 |
| ✓ Economic Systems | 4 |
| ✓ Conflict Resolution | 3 |

## Notes & Reflections

Each discipline plans its topics and content in isolation from the other disciplines. For example, the Language Arts teacher lists the typical topics for a semester. The sequence and time allotment is determined by the individual teacher using individual criteria while sifting out curricular priorities; "selectively abandoning"* or "judiciously including"* material in curricular designing.

*Art Costa, "Orchestrating the Second Wave"; *Cogitare*, Vol. V, No. 2, 1991.

*Think back. Select one discipline and list six priority units or topics. Then rank them according to overall curricular requirements.*

## ► Think Back: Re-Design ◄

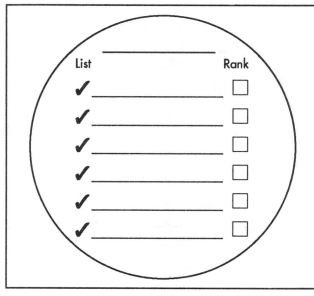

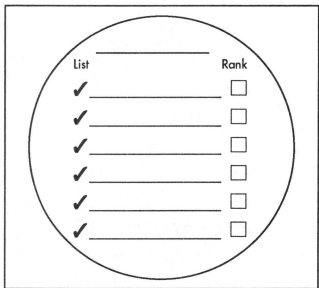

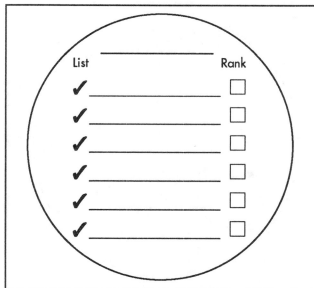

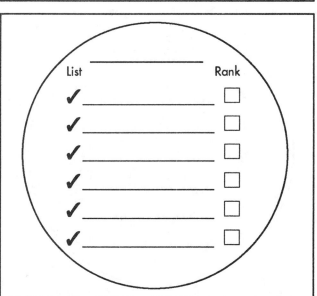

## Notes & Reflections

*Think ahead. List the **concepts** (rather than the topics or units) for an upcoming semester. Then rank the concepts according to curricular requirements.*

# ► Think Ahead:  Design  ◄

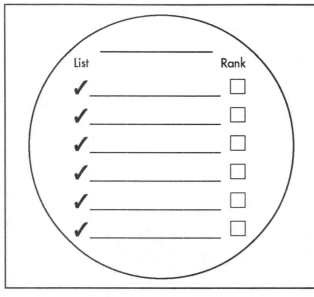

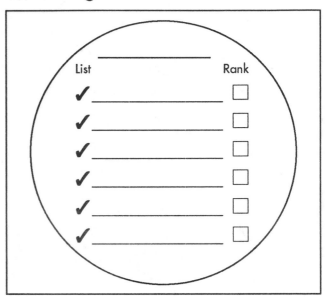

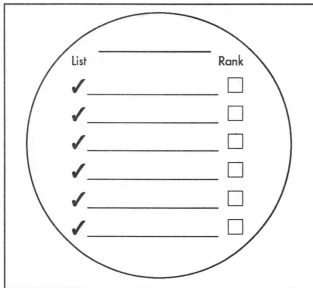

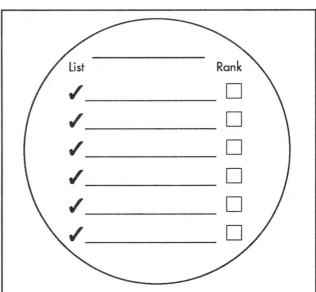

## Notes & Reflections

*Think again. List curricular priorities by topic, then rank by concepts. Refine the list as you go.*

# ► Think Again: Design ◄

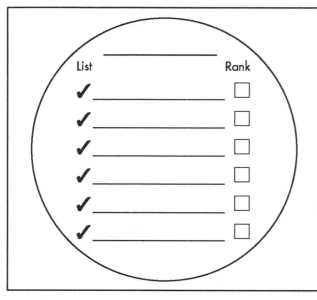

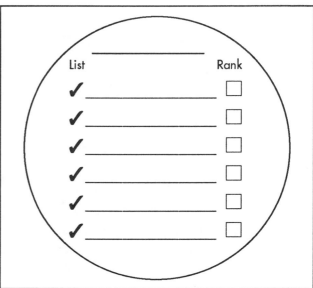

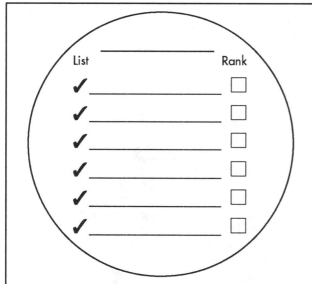

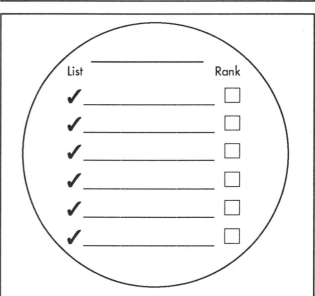

## Notes & Reflections

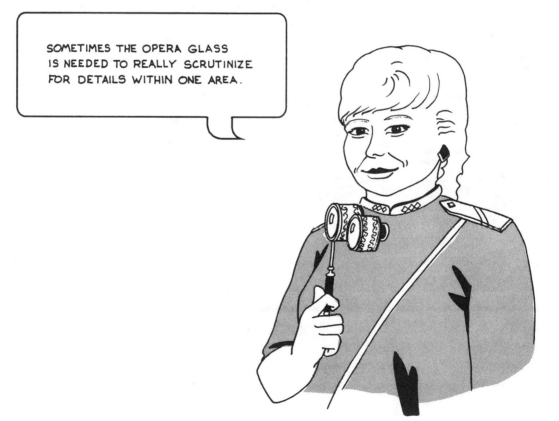

# Model

# 2

## CONNECTED

*Within each subject area, course content is connected topic to topic, concept to concept, one year's work to the next, and relates idea(s) explicitly.*

Opera glass—details of one discipline; focus on subtleties and interconnections

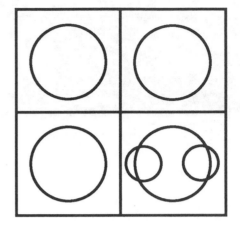

*"The object of education is to prepare the young to educate themselves throughout their lives."*
—Robert Maynard Hutchins

## What Is The Connected Model?

While the major discipline areas remain separate, this curricular model focuses on making explicit connections within each subject area, connecting one topic to the next; connecting one concept to another; connecting a skill to a related skill; connecting one day's work to the next, or even one semester's ideas to the next. The key to this model is the effort to deliberately relate curricula within the discipline rather than assuming that students will understand the connections automatically.

## What Does It Look Like?

Within the primary/elementary curriculum, for example, a relationship is drawn between the rock unit and the simple machines unit as students explicitly connect these while simultaneously seeing them as two distinct science areas: one is Earth Science and the other is Physical Science—both considered part of the sciences per se. By labeling for students the broad terms (in this case, Earth Science and Physical Science), students can begin to define the sciences for themselves by using these as organizational umbrellas. This becomes a first critical step in their understanding and conceptualization of the sciences as a realm of knowing.

Likewise, in a junior high or secondary school setting, the Earth Science teacher relates the Geology unit to the Astronomy unit by associating the evolutionary nature of each. The

---

**EXAMPLE:**

**Teacher relates the concept of fractions to decimals, which in turn relates to money, grades, etc.**

similarities between the two units become organizers for students as they work through both units to see that they can make explicit interrelationships.

## What Does It Sound Like?

The student sees connections between subject areas that have traditionally been taught separately. Here is the testimony of one former student, Eric J. Lerner:

> "I found there was a big difference between what excited me, trying to understand the universe, and what went on in our physics classes . . . I was bothered by logical contradictions in some of the things we were taught . . . Eventually, I reached the point where I could no longer accept the Second Law of Thermodynamics," Lerner recalled.

> Roughly, that concept holds that energy levels in a physical system tend to even out. For instance, introduce a bit of heat into a cold room and it disperses throughout the space, quickly becoming indistinguishable. "On a larger scale, the Second Law of Thermodynamics seems to reinforce the Big Bang theory," Lerner explained. "At the moment of creation, all energy was supposedly concentrated at one point and the universe was highly organized. Ever since, its energy has been dispersing as the universe degenerates into less and less organized states."

Eric goes on to relate the moment when he made the connection.

> "Then I grasped that biology contradicts the Second Law of Thermodynamics," Lerner said. "Consider evolution: living forms have gone from the less complex, like single-cell creatures, to the more complex, like human beings. Why should our planet be an exception? I asked myself. That made me realize there is something fundamentally wrong with the Big Bang theory and its conception that the universe is running down."*

The teacher can facilitate such connections in students' thinking by explicitly making links between subject areas.

## What Are The Advantages?

By connecting ideas within a discipline, the learner has the advantage of the big picture as well as a focused study of one aspect. In addition, key concepts are developed over time for internalization by the learner. Connecting ideas within a discipline permits the learner to review, reconceptualize, edit, and assimilate ideas gradually and may facilitate transfer.

TEACHERS CAN HELP STUDENTS MAKE CONNECTIONS BY ASKING QUESTIONS THAT STRETCH IDEAS.

## What Are The Disadvantages?

The various disciplines in this model remain separated and appear unrelated even though connections are made explicit within the designated discipline. Teachers are not encouraged to work together in this model, so content remains the focus without stretching concepts and ideas *across* other disciplines. The concentrated efforts to integrate *within* the discipline overlook opportunities to develop more global relationships to other subjects.

## When Is This Connected Model Useful?

The connected model is useful as a beginning step toward an integrated curriculum. Teachers feel confident looking for connections within their own discipline. As they become adept at relating ideas within the discipline, it becomes easier to scout for connections across disciplines. Also, connection-making can be done collaboratively within department meetings—which is again, old and familiar ground that sets a safe climate for change. Starting teacher teams using this model within the department or grade level can be a fruitful strategy to prime the pump for more complex integration models later on.

BACK AT THE MINDFUL SCHOOL, OUR TEACHERS, SUE, BOB, TOM, AND MARIA START TO EXPLORE THE <u>CONNECTORS WITHIN</u> THEIR OWN SUBJECT AREAS.

THIS YEAR I WANT TO PRESENT THE UNITS SO THEY MAKE MORE SENSE TO THE STUDENTS. IT SEEMS LOGICAL TO INTRODUCE THE CONCEPT OF NEGATIVE NUMBERS AFTER THEY WORK WITH THE QUADRANTS IN GRAPHING.

TO HELP STUDENTS UNDERSTAND HOW EVERYTHING WE STUDY IN BIOLOGY IS RELATED TO THE THEORY OF EVOLUTION, I'LL HAVE THEM KEEP AN "EVOLUTION" NOTEBOOK. THEY CAN LOG IDEAS AS WE STUDY, READ, AND DISCUSS THE VARIOUS TOPICS.

TO GENERATE AN INTEGRATED UNDERSTANDING OF AMERICAN LITERATURE, I'M GOING TO HAVE STUDENTS CRITIQUE EACH OF THE AUTHORS WE READ THIS SEMESTER USING "THE AMERICAN DREAM" THEME. THIS WILL WEAVE A COMMON STRAND THROUGHOUT THE UNITS.

BY APPROACHING THE UNIT ON EARLY GREECE AND INTERTWINING GREEK DRAMA INTO THE SEMESTER WORK, STUDENTS WILL GET A STUDY IN HUMANITIES RATHER THAN DISCRETE STUDIES OF HISTORY AND LITERATURE. IT SHOULD PROVIDE A MORE ENDURING IMAGE OF THE ERA.

*Think of units, topics, or concepts within a discipline that you've just finished teaching and jot down a "connection."*

# ▶ Samples ◀

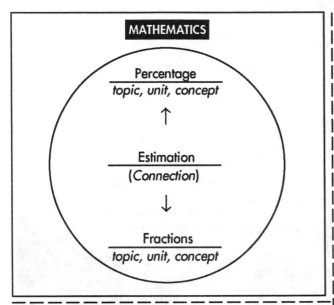

**MATHEMATICS**

Percentage
*topic, unit, concept*

↑

Estimation
*(Connection)*

↓

Fractions
*topic, unit, concept*

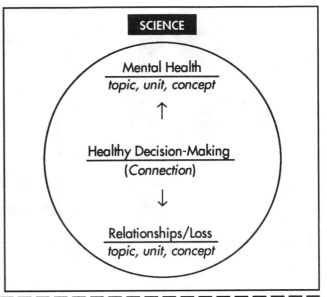

**SCIENCE**

Mental Health
*topic, unit, concept*

↑

Healthy Decision-Making
*(Connection)*

↓

Relationships/Loss
*topic, unit, concept*

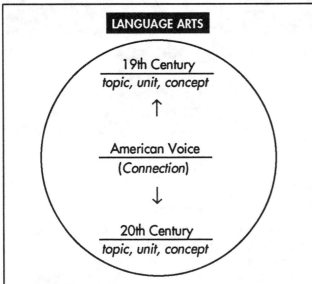

**LANGUAGE ARTS**

19th Century
*topic, unit, concept*

↑

American Voice
*(Connection)*

↓

20th Century
*topic, unit, concept*

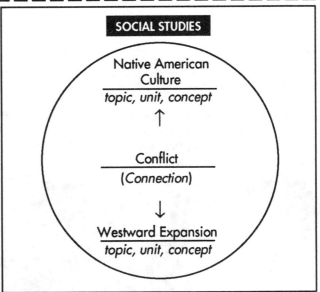

**SOCIAL STUDIES**

Native American Culture
*topic, unit, concept*

↑

Conflict
*(Connection)*

↓

Westward Expansion
*topic, unit, concept*

## Notes & Reflections

Each discipline connects particular topics, units, or concepts with connecting organizers. These frameworks provide common focal points for integrating ideas.

*Think back on units, topics, or concepts within a discipline that you've just taught. Jot down connections as you correlate them.*

# ▶ Think Back:  Re-Design ◀

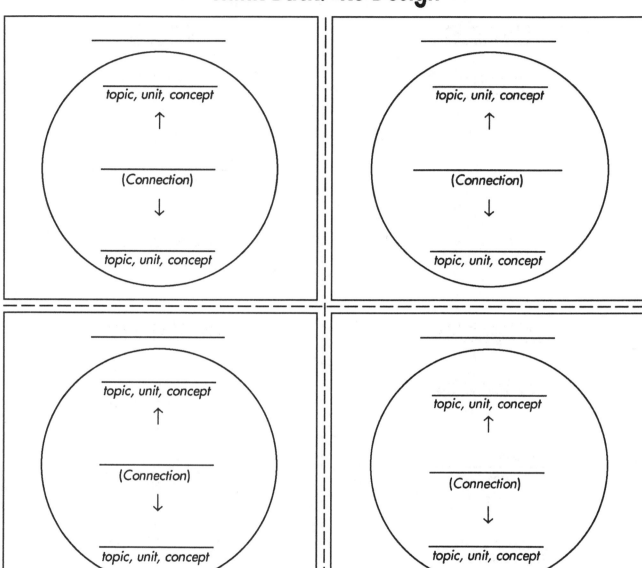

## Notes & Reflections

*Now, think ahead and try to connect ideas, topics, or concepts with units, topics, or concepts you plan to teach this semester.*

# ► Think Ahead:  Design ◄

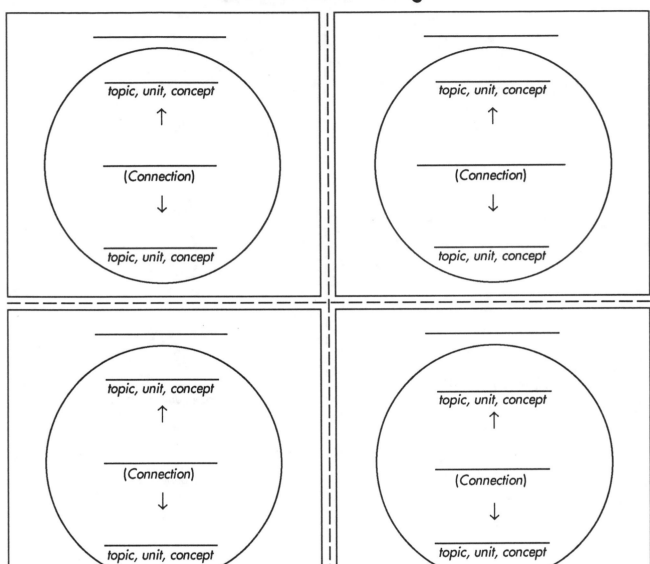

## Notes & Reflections

*Design or redesign units, topics, or concepts so they connect logically for lessons and learners.*

# ► Think Again: Design ◄

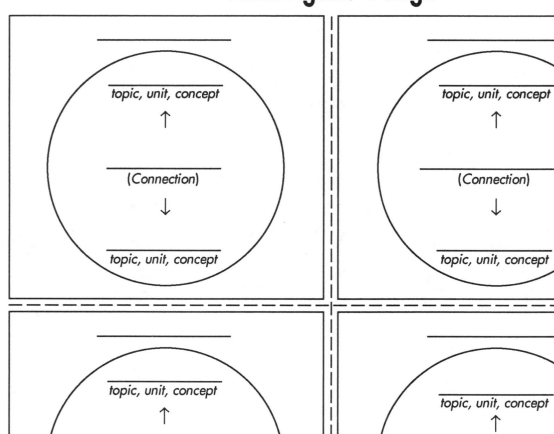

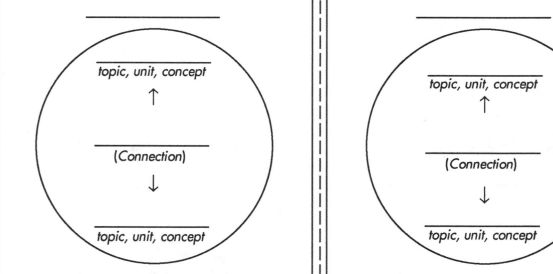

## Notes & Reflections

MANY TEACHERS "NEST"
A NUMBER OF IMPORTANT
IDEAS INTO A SINGLE
LESSON.

# Model 3

## NESTED

*Within each subject area, the teacher targets multiple skills: a social skill, a thinking skill, and a content-specific skill.*

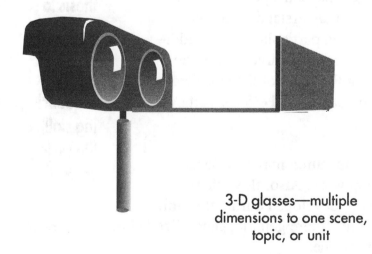

3-D glasses—multiple dimensions to one scene, topic, or unit

*"The business of education is not to make the young perfect in any one of the sciences, but to open and dispose their minds as may best make them capable of any, when they shall apply themselves to it."*
—John Locke

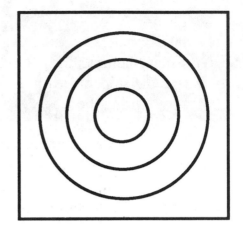

## What Is The Nested Model?

The nested model of integration is a rich design used by skilled teachers. They know how to get the most mileage from the lesson—any lesson. But, in this nested approach to instruction, careful planning is needed to structure multiple targets for student learning. However, nested integration takes advantage of natural combinations so the task seems pretty easy.

## What Does It Look Like?

An elementary content lesson on the circulatory system targets the concept of "systems" as well as facts and understanding on the circulatory system in particular. But, in addition to this conceptual target, the teacher also targets a thinking skill of cause and effect. Throughout the study of the circulatory system, students will be focusing on causes and effects as they pertain to the circulatory system.

In addition, a social skill such as cooperation may be a focal point as the class learns about group work. Also, flow-chart design may be an organizational skill developed during this unit. So, as the teacher "covers the content," more generic, generalized skills are "nested" together to enhance the learning experience.

### EXAMPLE:

**Teacher designs the unit on photosynthesis to simultaneously target consensus seeking (social skill), sequencing (thinking skill), and plant life cycle (science content).**

A high school lesson in the Computer Science class targets the Computer Assisted Drawing/ Computer Assisted Manufacturing (CAD/CAM) programs. Yet, as the students learn the actual workings of the program, the teacher has targeted the thinking skill of "envisioning" for explicit exploration and practice. In this "nested" approach, students are also instructed in ergonomics as they design furniture for schools of the future. Thus, the teacher clusters several skills in this nested model of integrating the curricula.

WHEN YOU THINK ABOUT IT, ANY LESSON CAN BE SET UP TO INCORPORATE THE NESTED MODEL.

## What Does It Sound Like?

STUDENT #1: Teachers used to be pretty predictable. They would tell you what you were supposed to know and then test you on it.

STUDENT #2: Yeah! I know what you mean. It was easy to psych out the test questions because the stuff was repeated eighteen times in class.

STUDENT #1: But now, they expect *you* to sort out what's important. And they want you to tell them how you figure things out.

STUDENT #2: That's not all. My teacher watches our "social behavior," too. She says our thinking and our behavior are just as important as our answers. This is getting out of control.

STUDENT #1: Yeah! They're getting too much mileage out of one lousy lesson.

## What Are The Advantages?

The pluses of the nested model are obvious to the veteran teacher. By nesting and clustering a number of objectives in the learning experience, student learning is enriched and enhanced. Typically, focusing on content, thinking strategies, social skills, and other serendipitous ideas, the single lesson takes on multiple dimensions. In this day and age of information overload, over-crowded curricula, and tight schedules, the experienced teacher may seek out fertile lessons that lay the groundwork for learning in multiple areas. While the nested model provides the needed attention to several areas of interest at once, it does not require the added burden of finding time to work and plan with another teacher. With this model, a single teacher can provide extensive integration of curricula.

## What Are The Disadvantages?

The possible disadvantages of the nested model arise from its very nature. Nesting two, three, or four learning targets into a single lesson may confuse students if the nesting is not executed carefully. The conceptual priorities of the lesson may become obscure because students are directed to perform many learning tasks at once.

## When Is This Nested Model Useful?

The nested model is most appropriate to use as teachers try to infuse thinking skills and cooperative skills into their content lessons. Keeping the content objectives in place, while adding a thinking focus and targeting social skills, will enhance the overall learning experience. Nesting particular skills in these three areas integrates concepts and attitudes easily through structured activities.

MEANWHILE, BACK AT THE MINDFUL SCHOOL, OUR TEACHERS IN THEIR DIFFERENT DEPARTMENTS ARE GETTING A LOT OF MILEAGE OUT OF THEIR LESSONS — THEY'RE TARGETING SOCIAL SKILLS, THINKING SKILLS, AND CONTENT SKILLS WITHIN A SINGLE LESSON.

I LIKE THIS IDEA OF "NESTED" SKILLS AS A WAY TO INTEGRATE. IT KEEPS MY DISCIPLINE PURE AND INTACT, YET I EXTEND THE LESSON INTO OTHER REALMS. IN GLOBAL STUDIES, I CAN USE DEBONO'S SIX THINKING HATS FOR "POINT OF VIEW" OF CURRENT EVENTS. WITH A JIGSAW MODEL, I CAN TALK ABOUT STUDENT RESPONSIBILITY.

GOOD IDEA, TOM! AND WHEN I INTRODUCE THE PERIODIC TABLE OF ELEMENTS, I COULD FOCUS ON THE CONTENT OF THE CHART, AND THEN TRY NESTING A FEW OTHER SKILLS AND CONCEPTS SUCH AS PATTERNS, SYMBOLS, OR MEMORY TECHNIQUES.

WHILE READING THE NOVEL THE OLD MAN AND THE SEA, I CAN FOCUS ON AUTHOR STYLE AND USE OF LANGUAGE AS I HAVE IN THE PAST. BUT I CAN ALSO TARGET THE CONCEPTS OF PERSEVERANCE AND FRIENDSHIP. ALSO, THE IDEA OF EMPHASIZING TEAMWORK AS A SOCIAL SKILL LOOKS POSSIBLE.

FOR EXAMPLE, IN A MATH LESSON, WHEN I AM TEACHING THE SKILL OF GRAPHING INFORMATION, I CAN ALSO EMPHASIZE PREDICTION OF THE LINE. I COULD USE THE IDEA OF NESTING, AND REQUIRE CONSENSUS IN THE GROUP FOR THEIR PREDICTIONS.

*Using a content piece as the first target, two other instructional focal points are designated that can be nested in a single lesson or unit of study.*

# ► Samples ◄

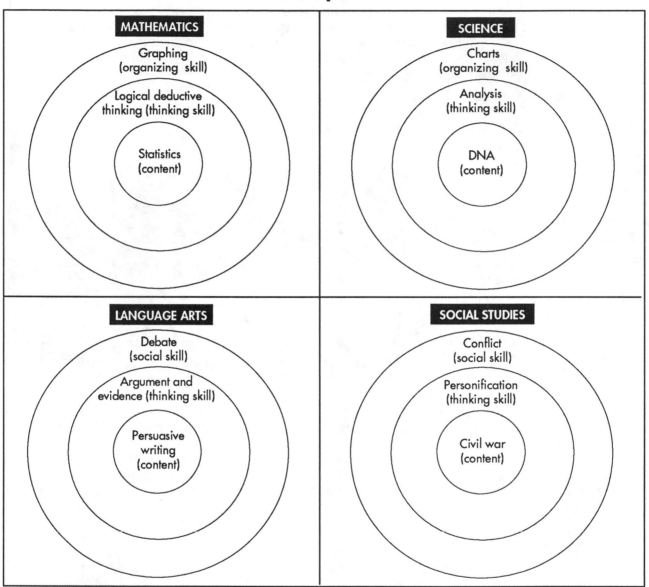

## Notes & Reflections

Within a content, the teacher uses the subject matter as the frame for a number of skills, concepts, and attitudes. The topic or unit provides the vehicle to carry along learning in related areas.

*Think back to something you just taught. Select a topic, unit, or concept from the content. Then add two other concepts or skills as further instructional targets.*

# ► Think Back: Re-Design ◄

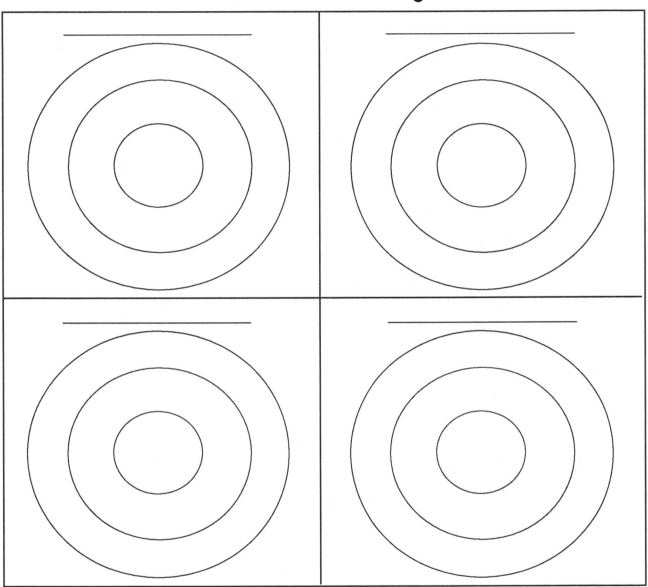

## Notes & Reflections

*Think ahead to upcoming units or topics. Select a content target first. Then select two other skills or concepts as additional instructional targets.*

# ▶ Think Ahead: Design ◀

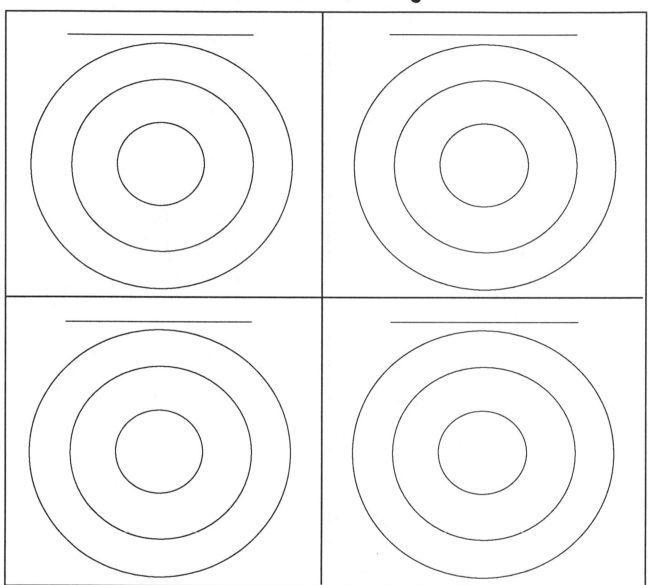

## Notes & Reflections

*Think again. Jot down the content topics or unit. Then target several other concepts or skills for explicit instruction within the same lesson(s).*

## ▶ Think Again: Design ◀

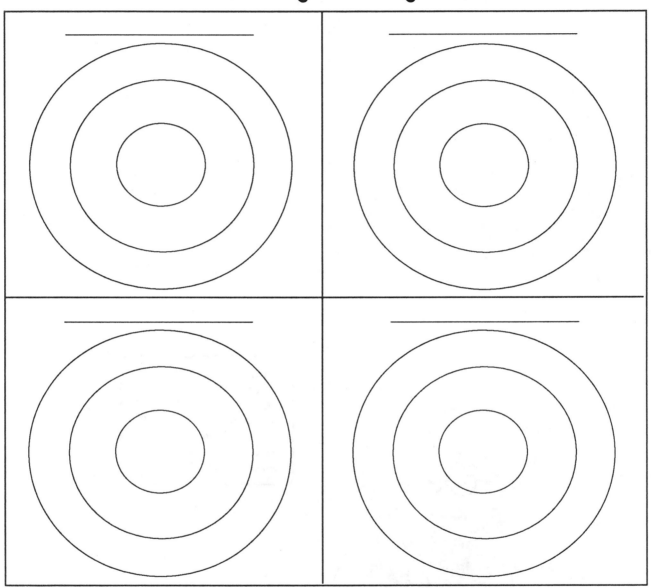

## Notes & Reflections

THIS IS THE FIRST
MODEL THAT HAS
TEACHERS REACH
ACROSS DEPARTMENTS
TO PLAN AND
SEQUENCE SOME
SIMILAR IDEAS.

# Model 4

# SEQUENCED

*Topics or units of study are rearranged and sequenced to coincide with one another. Similar ideas are taught in concert while remaining separate subjects.*

Eyeglasses—varied internal content framed
by broad, related concepts

*"Education is the transmission of civilization."*
—Will and Ariel Durant

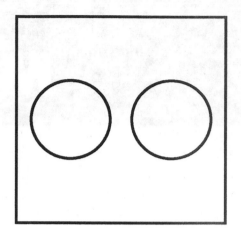

## What Is The Sequenced Model?

With limited articulation across disciplines, teachers can rearrange the order of their topics so that similar units coincide with each other. Two related disciplines can be sequenced so that the subject matter content of both are taught in parallel. By sequencing the order in which topics are taught, the activities of each enhance the other. In essence, one subject carries the other and vice versa.

## What Does It Look Like?

In the self-contained classroom, *Charlotte's Web* can accompany the unit on spiders. *Johnny Tremain* can parallel the study of the Revolutionary War. The graphing unit can coincide with data collection in the weather unit.

A secondary situation might sequence the study of the stock market in Math with the study of the Depression in History. Both domestic and global events can be used to parallel various units in the various subjects. In this way, current, relevant topics become the catalyst to study historic foundations, related mathematical concepts, or appropriate literary references.

EXAMPLE:

**English teacher presents an historical novel depicting a particular period while the History teacher teaches that same historical period.**

## What Does It Sound Like?

John Adams once said, "The textbook is not a moral contract that teachers are obliged to teach—teachers are obliged to teach children." Unfortunately, more often than one cares to admit, teachers follow the format and/or layout of the texts, going from the front of the book to the back. While this may work well in some cases, it might make more sense to rearrange the sequence of the units in other cases. The new sequence may be more logical if it parallels subject matter content *across* disciplines. When learners are given the advantage of seeing these natural connections across content, both the students and the teachers benefit. Learning becomes more generalized and therefore more easily transferred.

## What Are The Advantages?

The teacher, by rearranging the sequence of topics, chapters, and units, can dictate the curricular priorities rather than having to follow the sequence established by the editorial staff of the textbook. In this way, teachers can make the critical decisions about content. From the students' point of view, the deliberate sequencing of related topics across disciplines helps them make sense of their studies in both subject and content areas. Once again, integration aids transfer. When students see teachers in different content areas, in different rooms, in different periods, making similar points, their learning is reinforced in a powerful and meaningful way.

## What Are The Disadvantages?

A drawback of sequenced curricula is the compromise required to shape their model. Teachers must give up autonomy in making curriculum sequences as they partner with others. Also, to sequence according to current events requires ongoing collaboration and extreme flexibility on the part of all content-area people involved. This is not as easy as it sounds. However, in a very short time, even with only one afternoon together, teacher partners can easily do some rearranging and sequencing as a beginning step. If this first attempt at correlating two subject areas works, the two teachers can try sequencing more units for parallel teaching.

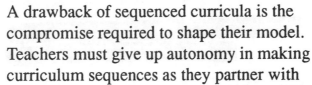

JUST BY REARRANGING THE ORDER OF TOPICS, TEACHERS CAN HELP KIDS MAKE THOSE CRITICAL CONNECTIONS.

## When Is This Sequenced Model Useful?

The sequenced model is useful in the beginning stages of the integration process, using two discipline areas that are easily tied to each other. The teacher, working with a partner, starts by listing curricular content separately. Then, the team tries to juggle the separate content pieces around until the two can "match up" or sequence some things to coincide. They try to parallel their different contents to make more sense to the students who are learning from both. In this model, both disciplines stay pure. Specific emphasis is still in the domain of the subject matter, but the student reaps the benefits of related content.

BY NOW, TEACHERS AT THE MINDFUL SCHOOL ARE BEGINNING TO SEE THE ADVANTAGES OF MAKING CONNECTIONS FOR BOTH LESSONS AND LEARNERS. A COUPLE OF THEM START TALKING ABOUT DOING SOME <u>PLANNING TOGETHER.</u>

AS WE AGREED TO DO IN OUR LAST FACULTY MEETING, BOB, I'VE LISTED THE KEY UNITS I WILL COVER THIS SEMESTER IN THE USUAL ORDER.

YES, I AGREE. THAT WOULD BE EASY FOR ME TO ADJUST AND I LIKE THE IDEA OF REINFORCEMENT OF THE CONCEPTS IN MATH CLASS.

GREAT, SUE! I DID A SIMILAR LIST. NOW, LET'S LOOK AT OUR LISTS TOGETHER AND SEE IF THERE'S A LOGICAL SEQUENCING SO THE TWO LISTS HAVE MORE MATCH UP FOR STUDENTS.

I NOTICE YOU'VE LISTED YOUR POLLUTION STUDY. I HAVE SOMETHING SIMILAR WITH MY LITERATURE UNIT ON PROJECTING FUTURE PROBLEMS. MAYBE WE COULD PLAN SOME FILMS OR FIELD EXPERIENCES TOGETHER.

YOU KNOW, MARIA, THAT DOES MAKE A LOT OF SENSE. I'M REALLY GLAD WE STARTED LOOKING AT ALL THIS. IT'S REFRESHING TO JUGGLE THINGS AROUND SOMETIMES.

Two teachers from different disciplines list five topics each.
Then they sequence them to parallel their teaching.

# ▶ Samples ◀

subject

subject

## Sequence

1. Robin Hood

2. The Midnight Ride of Paul Revere

3. The Slave Who Bought His Freedom

4. Nellie Bly

5. Diary of Anne Frank

## Sequence

1. Medieval times

2. American Revolution

3. Civil War

4. Women's Suffrage Movement

5. World War II

## List

✓ Robin Hood

✓ Nellie Bly

✓ Diary of Anne Frank

✓ The Midnight Ride of Paul Revere

✓ The Slave Who Bought His Freedom

## List

✓ Am. Hist.–Revolutionary War

✓ Am. Hist.–Civil War

✓ Am. Hist.–Womens' suffrage

✓ World Hist.–Medieval Times

✓ World War II

Barbara Bengston, Carpentersville, IL

## Notes & Reflections

Sequencing units with another teacher is an easy way to ensure that students make connections.

*Think back to two disciplines and list five topics for each. Then, working together, sequence across both disciplines for a logical order.*

# ▶ Think Back: Re-Design ◀

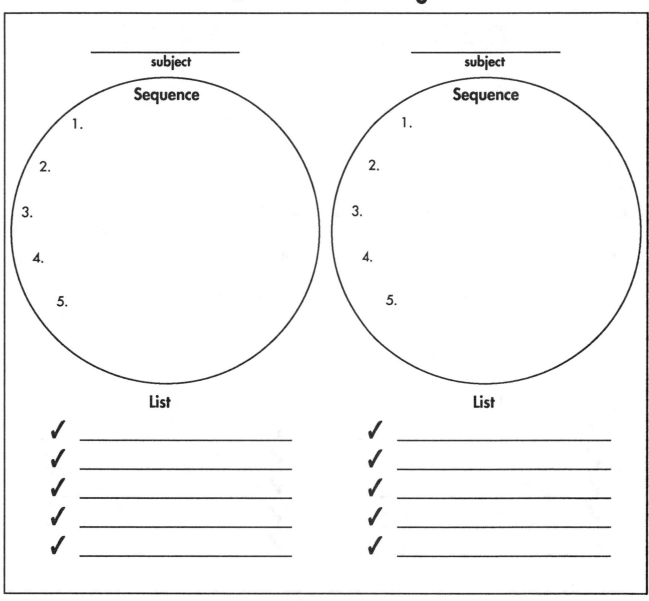

subject

**Sequence**

1.

2.

3.

4.

5.

**List**

✔ _____
✔ _____
✔ _____
✔ _____
✔ _____

subject

**Sequence**

1.

2.

3.

4.

5.

**List**

✔ _____
✔ _____
✔ _____
✔ _____
✔ _____

## Notes & Reflections

*Think ahead and list the content for two disciplines that will be coming up. Then, sequence the topics or units to parallel each other logically.*

# ▶ Think Ahead: Design ◀

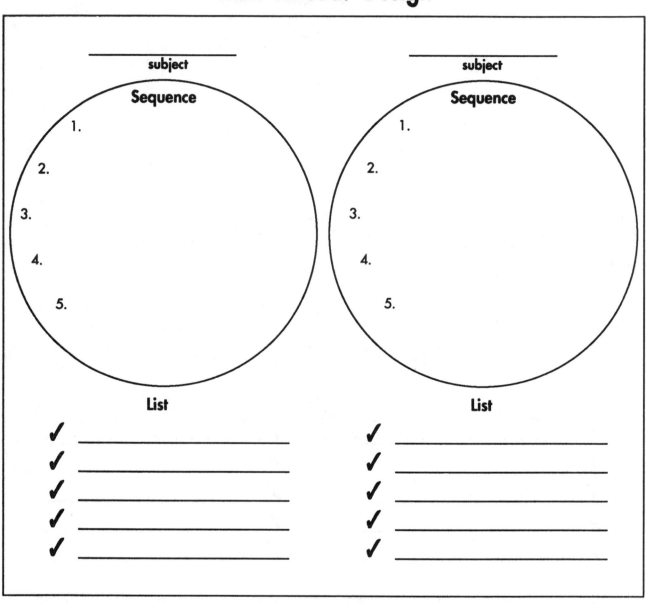

_____ subject

**Sequence**

1.

2.

3.

4.

5.

**List**

✔ _____
✔ _____
✔ _____
✔ _____
✔ _____

_____ subject

**Sequence**

1.

2.

3.

4.

5.

**List**

✔ _____
✔ _____
✔ _____
✔ _____
✔ _____

## Notes & Reflections

*Think again. List subject matter content across two disciplines. Then reorder the topics or units in a logical sequence.*

# ▶ Think Again: Design ◀

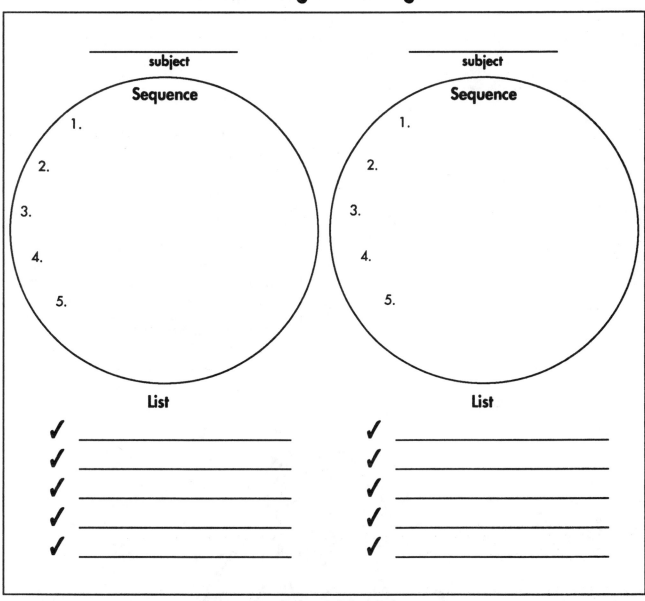

subject

subject

**Sequence**

1.

2.

3.

4.

5.

**List**

✓ _____

✓ _____

✓ _____

✓ _____

✓ _____

**Sequence**

1.

2.

3.

4.

5.

**List**

✓ _____

✓ _____

✓ _____

✓ _____

✓ _____

## Notes & Reflections

# Model 5

## SHARED

*Shared planning and teaching take place in two disciplines in which overlapping concepts or ideas emerge as organizing elements.*

Binoculars—two disciplines
that share overlapping
concepts and skills

*"The chief object of education is not to learn things, but to unlearn things."* —G. K. Chesterton

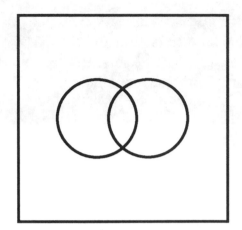

## What Is The Shared Model?

Certain broad disciplines create encompassing curricular umbrellas: Math and Science paired as sciences; Literature and History coupled under the label of the Humanities; Art, Music, Dance, and Drama viewed as the Fine Arts, and Computer Technology, Industrial and Home Arts embraced as the Practical Arts. Within these complementary disciplines, partner planning and/or teaching create a focus on shared concepts, skills, and attitudes.

## What Does It Look Like?

Cross-departmental partners plan a unit of study at the middle and secondary school levels. The two members of the team approach the preliminary planning session with a notion of key concepts, skills, and attitudes traditionally taught within the single-subject approach. As the pair identify their respective priorities, they look for overlaps in subject matter content. For example, the Literature teacher may focus on the concept of "the American Dream" as an organizer for a collection of short stories by American authors. At the same time, the History teacher notes that his unit on American History, that focuses on a study of each of the decades, could also use "the American Dream" as a unifying theme.

EXAMPLE:

**Science and Math teachers use data collection, charting, and graphing as shared concepts that can be team-taught.**

The shared curricula model is based on shared ideas that come from within the disciplines. This model differs radically from the thematic approach in the conceptualization of the unifying concepts because the concepts result from shared elements rather than the introduction of a theme from the outside. This is what the Venn diagram represents—similarities in the overlapped section. The key is to look for commonalities of both curricula.

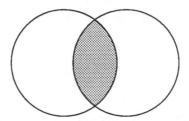

To use the shared view of curricular integration, the teacher needs to explore two disciplines for mutual concepts, skills, and/or attitudes as well as for actual content overlaps. This process is more complex than simply sequencing units to coincide with another subject area.

## What Does It Sound Like?

Elementary models of shared curricula embody standard planning models already in wide use. The self-contained classroom teacher plans the science unit on simple machines and the social studies unit on the industrial revolution around the concept of efficiency models. The shared concept of efficiency becomes the organizing umbrella. Teachers ask each other questions such as: "What concepts do these units share?", "Are we teaching similar skills?", and "Do the two units have commonalities in terms of concepts and ideas?"

## What Are The Advantages?

Advantages of this model of shared curriculum planning rest in the ease of using this as an early step toward more fully integrated models encompassing the four major disciplines. By coupling similar disciplines, the overlaps facilitate deep learning of concepts for transfer. Simply put, it's easier to schedule common planning periods for a two-teacher team than it is to juggle the scheduling for a four-teacher team. In addition, planning often leads to shared instructional experiences such as a film or field trip, because the two teachers can put their two periods together to create a larger time block.

## What Are The Disadvantages?

A barrier to shared curricula is the planning time needed to develop the models. In addition to the time, flexibility and compromise are essential ingredients for successful implementation—it requires both trust and teamwork. This model of integration across two disciplines requires commitment from the partners to work through the initial phases. To find real overlaps in curricular concepts requires in-depth dialogue and conversation.

## When Is This Shared Model Useful?

The shared curricula model is appropriate when subject matters are clustered into broad bands such as the Humanities or Practical Arts. Also, this model facilitates early stages of implementation toward integrated curricula. It is a viable model to use with two disciplines as an intermediary step to the four-discipline teams which are much more complicated and complex.

TEACHERS AT THE MINDFUL SCHOOL DISCUSS POSSIBILITIES FOR SOME SHARED CURRICULAR INTEGRATION IN THE FORM OF <u>CROSS-DEPARTMENTAL PARTNERSHIPS</u>. WORKING IN TEAMS OF TWO, THEY ARE DISCUSSING SOME PLANNING IDEAS.

I WAS INTRIGUED BY THE NUMBER OF STUDENTS LAST SEMESTER WHO MADE EXPLICIT CONNECTIONS BETWEEN WHAT YOU WERE DOING AND WHAT I WAS DOING. THE SEQUENCING REALLY SEEMED TO FOSTER THEIR INTEGRATION OF THE MATERIAL.

YOU KNOW, I HAD THE SAME EXPERIENCE. THERE REALLY WAS MUCH MORE NOTICE OF THE SIMILAR CONTENTS THAN I EXPECTED. IN FACT, I NEVER REALLY THOUGHT THEY'D NOTICE AT ALL.

REMEMBER—I SUGGESTED LAST YEAR THAT WE MIGHT SHARE SOME FILMS AND FIELD EXPERIENCES. HOW WOULD YOU FEEL ABOUT TRYING ONE SHORT UNIT NEXT SEMESTER, SAY, THREE WEEKS LONG?

I'M WILLING TO TRY ONE IF IT IS WELL PLANNED AND DOESN'T TAKE TOO MUCH TIME. DID YOU HAVE ONE UNIT IN PARTICULAR IN MIND?

*Two disciplines that seem to have natural relationships are*
*scrutinized for concepts and ideas that overlap.*

# ▶ Samples ◀

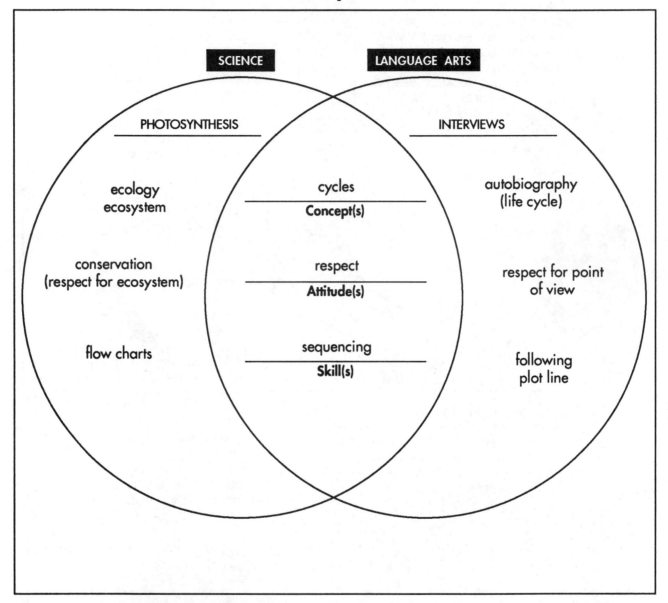

| SCIENCE | LANGUAGE ARTS |

**PHOTOSYNTHESIS**

ecology
ecosystem

conservation
(respect for ecosystem)

flow charts

cycles
_____
**Concept(s)**

respect
_____
**Attitude(s)**

sequencing
_____
**Skill(s)**

**INTERVIEWS**

autobiography
(life cycle)

respect for point
of view

following
plot line

# Notes & Reflections

Topics and units from two related disciplines offer rich possibilities for integration by
identifying basic concepts, skills, and attitudes that overlap.

*Think back to the units and topics taught last semester. With a partner, talk about concepts that overlap.*

# ► Think Back: Re-Design ◄

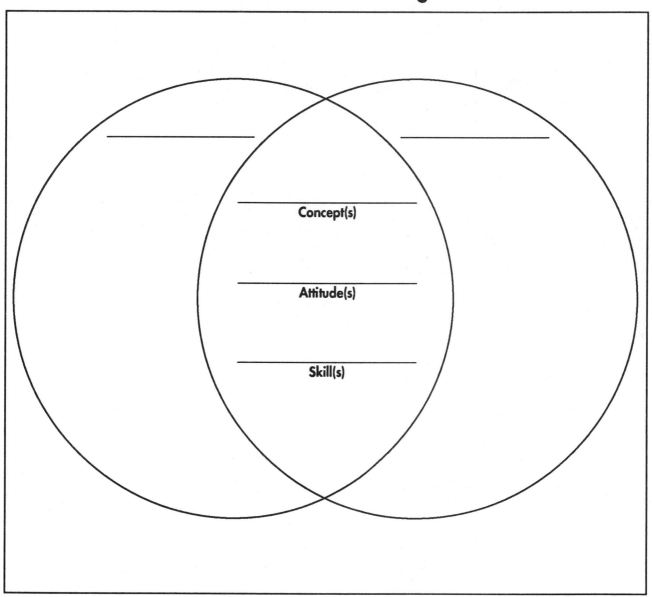

Concept(s)

Attitude(s)

Skill(s)

## Notes & Reflections

*Think ahead with a partner about the content across two disciplines. Sort out the concepts, skills, or attitudes that overlap.*

# ► Think Ahead: Design ◄

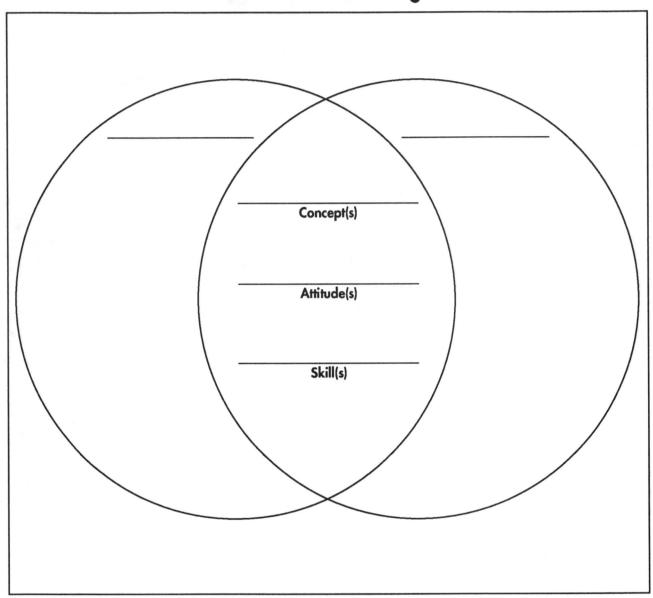

Concept(s)

Attitude(s)

Skill(s)

## Notes & Reflections

*Think again with a partner and form a different discipline. List the upcoming content and look for overlapping ideas that can be shared.*

# ▶ Think Again: Design ◀

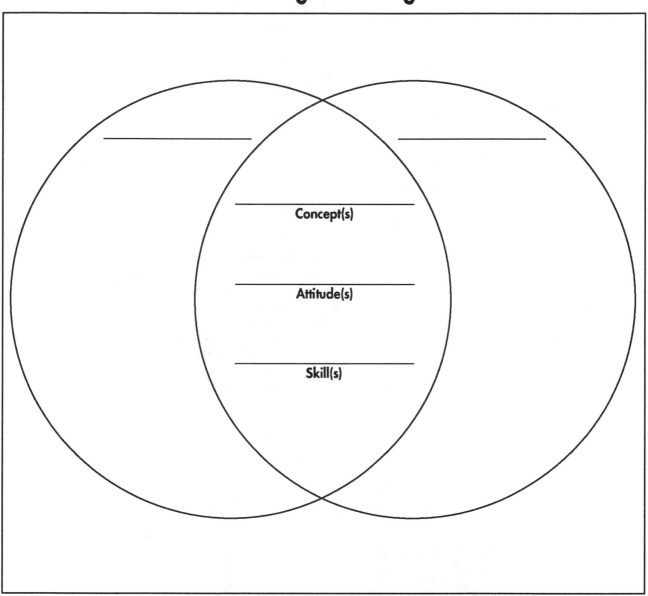

Concept(s)

Attitude(s)

Skill(s)

## Notes & Reflections

THIS IS THE MOST POPULAR MODEL OF INTEGRATION— THE WEBBED THEME. TEACHERS VIEW THE CURRICULA THROUGH A TELESCOPE FOR A PICTURE OF AN ENTIRE CONSTELLATION OF SUBJECTS AND ACTIVITIES.

# Model 6

# WEBBED

*A fertile theme is webbed to curriculum contents and disciplines; subjects use the theme to sift out appropriate concepts, topics, and ideas.*

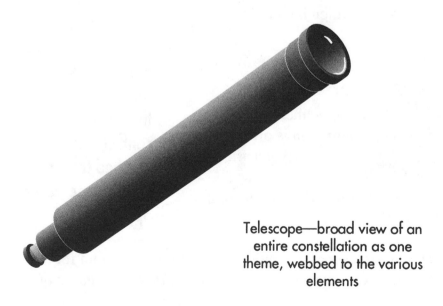

Telescope—broad view of an entire constellation as one theme, webbed to the various elements

*"We must open the doors of opportunity. But we must also equip our people to walk through those doors."*—Lyndon B. Johnson

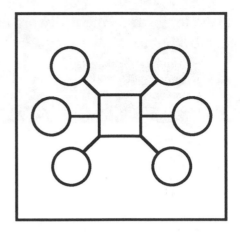

## What Is The Webbed Model?

Webbed curricula represent the thematic approach to integrating subject matter. Typically, this thematic approach to curriculum development begins with a theme such as "transportation" or "inventions." Once a cross-departmental team has made this decision, it uses the theme as an overlay to the different subjects: inventions lead to the study of simple machines in Science, reading and writing about inventors in Language Arts, designing and building models in Industrial Arts, drawing and studying Rube Goldberg contraptions in Math, making flow charts in computer technology classes. In more sophisticated webbings, intricate units of study can be developed in which integration occurs in all relevant areas.

## What Does It Look Like?

In departmentalized situations, the webbed curricular approach to integration is often achieved through the use of a fairly generic but fertile theme such as "patterns" or "cycles." This conceptual theme provides rich possibilities for the inherent diversities of the various disciplines.

EXAMPLE:

**Teacher presents a simple topical theme, such as the circus, and webs it to the subject areas. A conceptual theme, such as conflict, can be webbed for more depth in the theme approach.**

While similar conceptual themes such as *patterns* or *conflict* provide fertile ground for cross-disciplinary units of study, the elementary models can also use a *book* or a *genre of books* as the topic, to thematically organize their curricula. For example, *fairy tales* or *dog stories* can become catalysts for curricular webbing. Typical lists look like this . . .

| CONCEPTS | TOPICS | CATEGORIES |
|---|---|---|
| freedom | The individual and society | animal stories |
| cooperation | | biographies |
| challenge | Community relationships | adventure |
| conflict | | science fiction |
| discovery | The World Wars | the Renaissance |
| culture | | Medieval times |
| change | The Pacific Rim partnerships | the Impressionists |
| argument & evidence | | Great Books |
| perseverance | | |

## What Does It Sound Like?

When searching for a theme, teacher teams generally begin with an idea-gathering session that sounds like lots of genuine interaction, conversation, and dialogue among colleagues: "How 'bout this one?" "What do you think of this?" "I read about a school that used *cultural diversity* as an overriding theme." "Let's brainstorm a long list. I don't want to use the first one we think of just to be done with it." "Maybe we should ask the kids for their ideas." "I have some lists of theme ideas from a workshop." "Yeah, but we will need to look at that list carefully and compare them to some criteria. I have Perkins' criteria here."

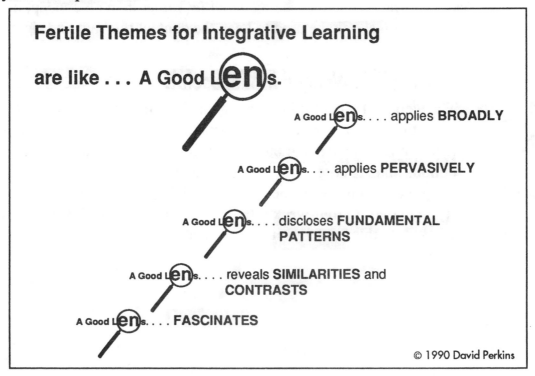

**Fertile Themes for Integrative Learning**

are like . . . A Good Lens.

A Good Lens. . . . applies **BROADLY**

A Good Lens. . . . applies **PERVASIVELY**

A Good Lens. . . . discloses **FUNDAMENTAL PATTERNS**

A Good Lens. . . . reveals **SIMILARITIES** and **CONTRASTS**

A Good Lens. . . . **FASCINATES**

© 1990 David Perkins

And so it goes as they explore possibilities and set guidelines for reaching a decision.

## What Are The Advantages?

An advantage of the webbed approach to curricular integration is the motivational factor that results from selecting high-interest themes. In addition, the webbed model or unit-writing approach is familiar to seasoned teachers and is a fairly straightforward curriculum planning model for less experienced teachers to grasp. It also facilitates teamwork planning as cross-departmental teams work to weave a theme into all content areas. The thematic approach or webbed model provides a visible and motivational umbrella for students. It is easy for them to see how different activities and ideas are connected.

## What Are The Disadvantages?

The most serious difficulty with the webbed model lies in the selection of a theme. There is a tendency to grab at shallow themes that are superficially useful in curriculum planning. Often these artificial themes lead to a contrived curriculum. Also, caution must be used not to sacrifice the logical and necessary scope and sequence inherent in the disciplines. In this model, teachers can get bogged down in curriculum writing that may not warrant the time involved as compared to long-term use of the thematic unit in years to come. (Usually a theme is *not* repeated.) Also, teachers can become focused on *activities* rather than on concept development in this model, so caution should be used to keep the content relevant and rigorous.

## When Is This Webbed Model Useful?

The webbed model for integrating curriculum is a team approach that takes time to develop. Summer curriculum writing time is an opportune moment to initiate this model so teachers can fully explore theme options and set criteria for quality. This model takes extensive planning and coordination among the various departments and special subject areas. It's a great model to use when trying a two- to four-week interdisciplinary pilot unit. Because of the intense planning needed to do this model well, it is advisable to start with a manageable piece of the curriculum.

AT THE STAFF MEETING AT THE MINDFUL SCHOOL, MARIA, TOM, BOB, AND SUE COMMIT TO DO A THREE-WEEK THEME...

I AM EXCITED ABOUT SELECTING A THEME THAT CAN BE WEBBED TO ALL THE CONTENTS. IT TAKES ME BACK TO MY COLLEGE DAYS, WHEN WE USED TO WRITE INTERDISCIPLINARY UNITS. THE PENDULUM DOES SWING, DOESN'T IT?

YOU KNOW, I HAD THE SAME THOUGHT. I THINK THIS DESIGN IS WORTHWHILE. IT WILL PULL WHAT WERE SEPARATE AND DISPARATE PARTS OF THE CURRICULUM TOGETHER FOR THE KIDS.

YES! REMEMBER THE ARTICLE WE READ ON "FINDING FERTILE THEMES"? THE CRITERIA SET FORTH BY PERKINS IN THAT PIECE SEEMED QUITE USEFUL. DO YOU REMEMBER WHAT THEY WERE?

I HAVE THE PERKINS ARTICLE HERE. LET'S BRAINSTORM SOME IDEAS AND "SELECTIVELY ABANDON" THE MORE SUPERFICIAL ONES. I HAVE TOO MANY PRIORITIES TO WASTE TIME. I WANT THE ACTIVITIES TO BE REALLY MEANINGFUL.

OK, LET'S SEE. IT LOOKS LIKE WE HAVE TWO CATEGORIES: TOPICAL THEMES AND CONCEPTUAL THEMES. LET'S SORT THAT OUT FIRST. THEN, ACCORDING TO PERKINS' CRITERIA, LOOK TO SEE IF THE THEME: 1. APPLIES BROADLY, 2. APPLIES PERSUASIVELY, 3. REVEALS ELEMENTAL PATTERNS, 4. PROVIDES SIMILARITIES AND CONTRASTS, AND 5. FASCINATES.

*A theme is designated as the central idea and used as an overlay to the various content areas for an interdisciplinary approach.*

## ► Samples ◄

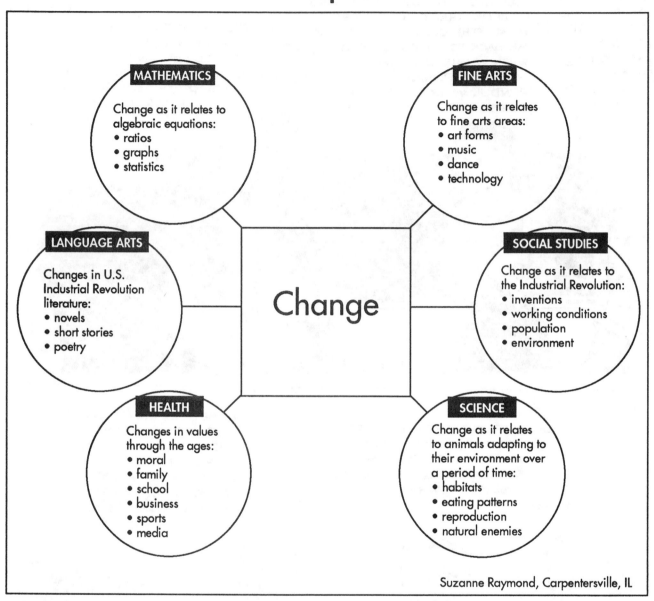

**MATHEMATICS**

Change as it relates to algebraic equations:
• ratios
• graphs
• statistics

**FINE ARTS**

Change as it relates to fine arts areas:
• art forms
• music
• dance
• technology

**LANGUAGE ARTS**

Changes in U.S. Industrial Revolution literature:
• novels
• short stories
• poetry

**Change**

**SOCIAL STUDIES**

Change as it relates to the Industrial Revolution:
• inventions
• working conditions
• population
• environment

**HEALTH**

Changes in values through the ages:
• moral
• family
• school
• business
• sports
• media

**SCIENCE**

Change as it relates to animals adapting to their environment over a period of time:
• habitats
• eating patterns
• reproduction
• natural enemies

Suzanne Raymond, Carpentersville, IL

## Notes & Reflections

In this webbed model, the theme provides a fresh lens with which to frame and view content. The theme acts as a common umbrella that is visible to students as they work in the various content areas. It's an easy integration model for the learner.

*Think back to units you've just done and, as an interdisciplinary team (or a grade level team), see if you can find a theme that might have worked for all of you.*

## ▶ Think Back: Re-Design ◀

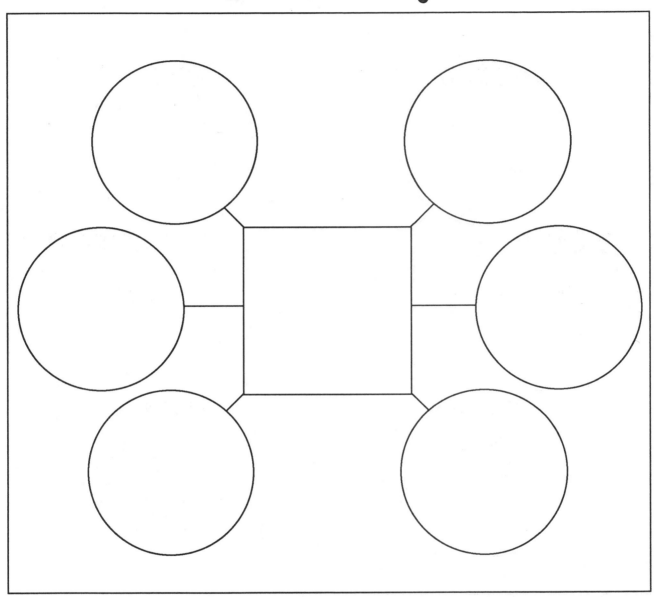

## Notes & Reflections

*Think ahead to next semester. As an interdisciplinary team (or a grade level team) select an umbrella theme to web with the various content areas.*

# ▶ Think Ahead: Design ◀

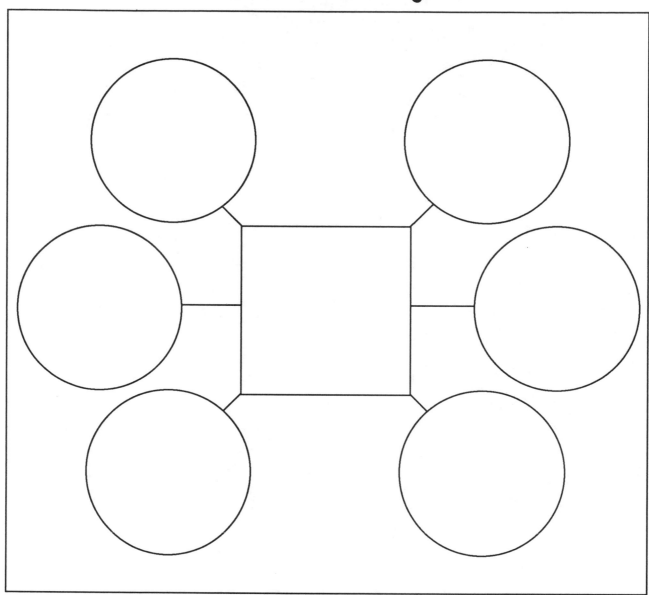

## Notes & Reflections

*Think again. Try another theme and outline the content for another unit of study.*

# ▶ Think Again: Design ◀

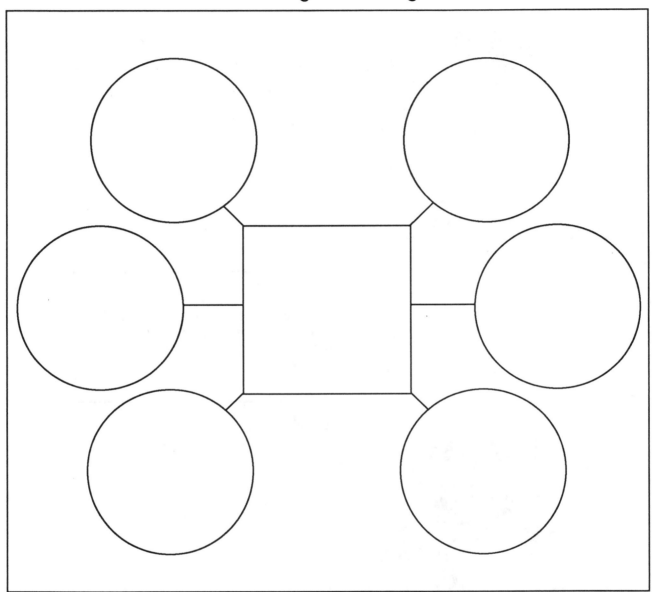

## Notes & Reflections

THE MAGNIFYING GLASS PROVIDES A VIEW OF THE BIG IDEA AS THE METACURRICULAR THREADS ARE ENLARGED.

# Model 7

# THREADED

*The metacurricular approach threads thinking skills, social skills, multiple intelligences, technology, and study skills through the various disciplines.*

Magnifying glass—big ideas
that magnify all content through
a metacurricular approach

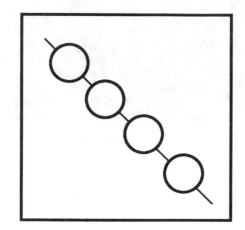

*"The great end of an education is to discipline rather than to furnish the mind. To train it to the use of its own powers rather than to fill it with the accumulation of others."*—Tryon Edwards

## What Is The Threaded Model?

Thinking skills (p. 65), social skills (p. 66), study skills, graphic organizers, technology, and a multiple intelligences (p. 67) approach to learning thread through all disciplines. This threaded model of curricular integration focuses on the metacurriculum that supersedes or intersects the very heart of any and all subject matter content. For example, prediction is a skill used to estimate in math, forecast in current events, anticipate in a novel, and hypothesize in the science lab. Consensus-seeking strategies are used in resolving conflicts in any problem-solving situation. These skills are, in essence, threaded through standard curricular content.

## What Does It Look Like?

Using the idea of a metacurriculum, grade-level or interdepartmental teams target a set of thinking skills to infuse into the existing content priorities. For example, using the "cluster curriculum" (see p. 65), the freshman team might choose the **analysis** cluster of thinking skills to infuse into each content: Science (classify), Social Studies (compare and contrast), Language Arts (attribute), Math (sequence). Likewise, social skills and the multiple intelligences can be threaded through the various disciplines.

**EXAMPLE:**

**Teaching staff targets prediction in Reading, Math, and Science lab experiments while Social Studies teacher targets forecasting current events, and thus threads the skill (prediction) across disciplines.**

## THE CLUSTER CURRICULUM OF THINKING SKILLS

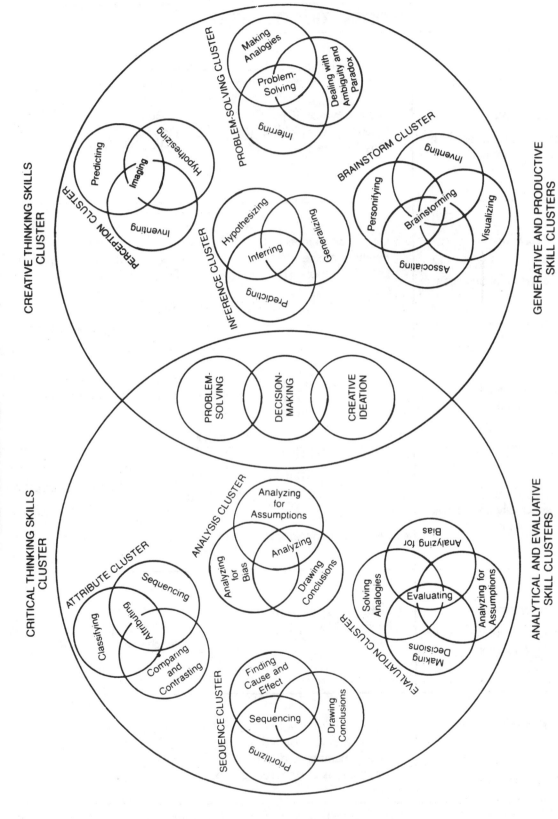

CREATIVE THINKING SKILLS CLUSTER

PROBLEM-SOLVING CLUSTER

Making Analogies

Problem-Solving

Dealing with Ambiguity and Paradox

Inferring

Predicting

Imaging

Hypothesizing

Inventing

PERCEPTION CLUSTER

BRAINSTORM CLUSTER

Inventing

Personifying

Brainstorming

Visualizing

Associating

INFERENCE CLUSTER

Hypothesizing

Inferring

Generalizing

Predicting

GENERATIVE AND PRODUCTIVE SKILL CLUSTERS

PROBLEM-SOLVING

DECISION-MAKING

CREATIVE IDEATION

CRITICAL THINKING SKILLS CLUSTER

ATTRIBUTE CLUSTER

Sequencing

Attributing

Classifying

Comparing and Contrasting

ANALYSIS CLUSTER

Analyzing for Assumptions

Analyzing for Bias

Analyzing

Drawing Conclusions

EVALUATION CLUSTER

Analyzing for Bias

Solving Analogies

Evaluating

Analyzing for Assumptions

Making Decisions

SEQUENCE CLUSTER

Finding Cause and Effect

Sequencing

Drawing Conclusions

Prioritizing

ANALYTICAL AND EVALUATIVE SKILL CLUSTERS

Balancing your choices from both critical and creative thinking, select a micro skill, a cluster of skills, or two clusters to work with as a department or grade level for the unit, the semester, or the year.

From *Teach Them Thinking: Mental Menus for 24 Thinking Skills*, Robin Fogarty and James Bellanca, Skylight Publishing, Inc., 1986.

Select appropriate social skills to target as a grade level, department, or interdisciplinary team.

| SOCIAL SKILLS OVERVIEW | |
|---|---|
| **PHASE** | **SOCIAL SKILLS**<br>Communication (C), Trust (T), Leadership (L), Conflict Resolution (CR) |
| **Forming**<br>to organize groups and establish behavior guidelines | Use a 6" voice. (C)　　　　Heads together. (C)<br>Listen to your neighbor. (C)　Do your job. (L)<br>Stay with the group. (C)　　Help each other. (L) |
| **Norming**<br>to complete assigned tasks and build effective relationships | Include all members. (L)　　Let all participate. (L)<br>Encourage others. (L)　　　Respect each other's opinions. (T)<br>Listen with focus. (T)　　　Stay on task. (L) |
| **Conforming**<br>to promote critical thinking and maximize the learning of all | Clarify. (C)　　　　　　　Probe for differences. (CR)<br>Paraphrase ideas. (C)　　　Generate alternatives. (CR)<br>Give examples. (C)　　　　Seek consensus. (CR) |
| **Storming**<br>to function effectively and enable the work of the team | Sense tone. (C)　　　　　　See all points of view. (CR)<br>Disagree with idea not<br>　person.(CR)　　　　　　Try to agree. (CR)<br>Keep an open mind. (T)　　Contribute own ideas. (L) |
| **Performing**<br>to foster higher-level thinking skills, creativity, and intuition | Elaborate on ideas. (C)　　Extend ideas. (C)<br>Integrate ideas. (L)　　　　Synthesize. (L)<br>Justify ideas. (CR)　　　　Reach consensus. (CR) |
| **Re-forming**<br>to apply across curriculum and transfer into life beyond the classroom | Begin cycle of social skills each time:<br>• New group is formed.　　　• New task is given.<br>• New member joins group.　• Long absenses occur.<br>• Member is absent from group. |

From *Blueprints For Thinking In The Cooperative Classroom*, James Bellanca and Robin Fogarty, Skylight Publishing, Inc., 1991, 2nd ed.

Select one or a set of intelligences to focus on in a unit of study or a single lesson.

**7**

WAYS OF KNOWING

MULTIPLE
INTELLIGENCES

## Logical/Mathematical Intelligence

Often called "scientific thinking," this intelligence deals with inductive and deductive thinking/reasoning, numbers, and the recognition of abstract patterns.

## Visual/Spatial Intelligence

This intelligence, which relies on the sense of sight and being able to visualize an object, includes the ability to create internal mental images/pictures.

## Body/Kinesthetic Intelligence

This intelligence is related to physical movement and the knowings/wisdom of the body, including the brain's motor cortex, which controls bodily motion.

## Musical/Rhythmic Intelligence

This intelligence is based on the recognition of tonal patterns, including various environmental sounds, and on a sensitivity to rhythm and beats.

## Verbal/Linguistic Intelligence

This intelligence, which is related to words and language (written and spoken) dominates most Western educational systems.

## Intrapersonal Intelligence

This intelligence relates to inner states of being, self-reflection, metacognition (i.e. thinking about thinking), and awareness of spiritual realities.

## Interpersonal Intelligence

This intelligence operates primarily through person-to-person relationships and communication.

From *Seven Ways of Knowing: Teaching for Multiple Intelligences*, David Lazear, Skylight Publishing, Inc. 1991.

## What Does It Sound Like?

As the thinking skills or social skills are threaded into the content, the teacher asks questions such as: "How did you think about that?", "What thinking skill did you find most helpful?", "How well did your group work today?", and "Have you used your musical intelligences today?" These processing questions contrast sharply to the usual cognitive questions such as, "What answer did you get?" and "How many agree?" (Sometimes, the above metacognitive questions sound to the kids like the teacher is "wasting time." Students will often say, "Ok, what do you really want us to do?").

## What Are The Advantages?

Advantages of the threaded model revolve around the concept of the metacurriculum. This metacurriculum is the awareness and control of the skills and strategies of thinking and learning that go beyond the subject matter content. Teachers stress the metacognitive behavior so students learn about *how* they are learning. By making students aware of the learning processes, future transfer is facilitated. The plus is that in this integration model, not only does the content stay pure for each discipline, but the students reap the added benefit of a superordinate kind of thinking that has transfer power for life skills.

## What Are The Disadvantages?

A disadvantage of the threaded model is the necessity of adding "another" curriculum. Content connections across subject matter are not addressed explicitly. The metacurriculum surfaces, but the disciplines remain static. Connections between and among the subject matter contents are not stressed. Also, in order to thread the metacurriculum through the content, all teachers need an understanding of those skills and strategies.

## When Is This Threaded Model Useful?

The threaded model is used to integrate curricula when a metacurriculum is a district focus. This model is appropriate to use as one of the alternative steps toward a more intense subject matter integration. The threaded model is easier to "sell" to hard-core curriculum advocates who are reluctant to shift the subject matter priorities. Therefore, this becomes a viable senior high model to start with as teachers keep their content intact and infuse thinking, cooperating, and multiple intelligences into that content.

THE MINDFUL SCHOOL TEACHERS FIND IT EASY TO THREAD CERTAIN SKILLS THROUGH THEIR PARTICULAR CONTENTS... MAKING INFERENCES IS THE THINKING SKILL TARGETED...

SO, OUR TEACHER TEAMS WILL FOCUS ON THE THINKING SKILL OF INFERENCING. IN PARTICULAR, THE SCIENCE CLASSES WILL TARGET INFERENCE AND OBSERVATION AS KEY SKILLS.

RIGHT, BOB. INFERRING FROM DATA AND PREDICTING TRENDS, BOTH IN THE HISTORICAL SENSE AND IN FUTURE STUDIES, ALSO HAS THE POTENTIAL TO ENRICH THE CURRICULUM CONTENT. AT FIRST, I WAS AFRAID THE SUBJECT MATTER CONTENT WOULD LOSE AND WE WOULD DILUTE THE DISCIPLINES, BUT THIS ACTUALLY IS ENHANCING MY CONTENT!

YOU KNOW MARIA, INFERRING FROM GRAPHS, CHARTS, AND DATA IS A NATURAL FOR MATH CLASS. WITH THE OVERLOAD OF INFORMATION AND THE INCREASED USE OF GRAPHICS, STUDENTS NEED WORK IN MAKING INFERENCES FROM THE GATHERED DATA. IT'S A RICH THREAD TO STRING THROUGH EVERYTHING WE DO.

READING BETWEEN THE LINES — MAKING INFERENCES IS AN ABSOLUTE BASIC EXPECTATION OF GOOD READERS. I THINK THE STUDY OF LITERATURE THIS SEMESTER CAN BE GREATLY ENRICHED. STUDENTS WILL BE EXPECTED TO GO BEYOND THE LITERAL INFORMATION PRESENTED.

*Interdisciplinary or grade-level teams target a thinking skill or cooperative skill, etc., and thread that skill through curricular content in all four disciplines.*

# ► Samples ◄

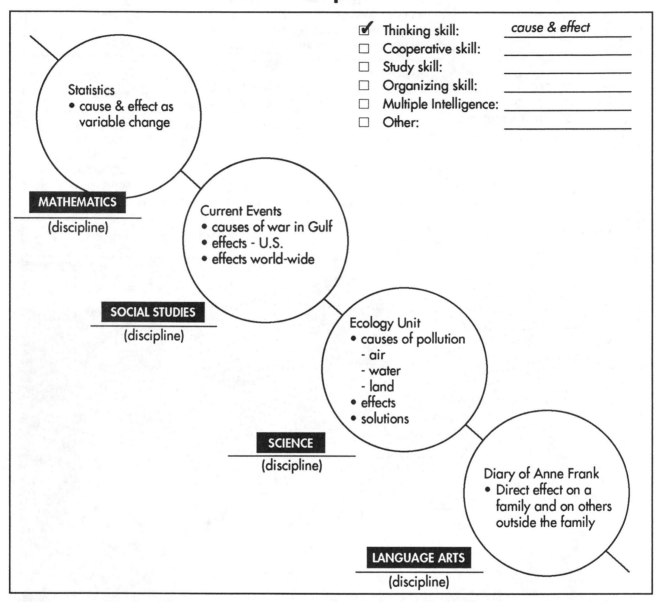

☑ Thinking skill: *cause & effect*
☐ Cooperative skill: _____
☐ Study skill: _____
☐ Organizing skill: _____
☐ Multiple Intelligence: _____
☐ Other: _____

Statistics
• cause & effect as variable change

**MATHEMATICS**
(discipline)

Current Events
• causes of war in Gulf
• effects - U.S.
• effects world-wide

**SOCIAL STUDIES**
(discipline)

Ecology Unit
• causes of pollution
  - air
  - water
  - land
• effects
• solutions

**SCIENCE**
(discipline)

Diary of Anne Frank
• Direct effect on a family and on others outside the family

**LANGUAGE ARTS**
(discipline)

## Notes & Reflections

Threading the thinking skill (or metacurriculum) through the subject matter content takes some consensus from the team members. However, there is no "watering down" of content in the respective disciplines. It's an amiable teaching model with positive outcomes for students.

*Think back to units the team members have recently taught. Identify some metacurricular skills that seem to enhance the content focus.*

# ► Think Back: Re-Design ◄

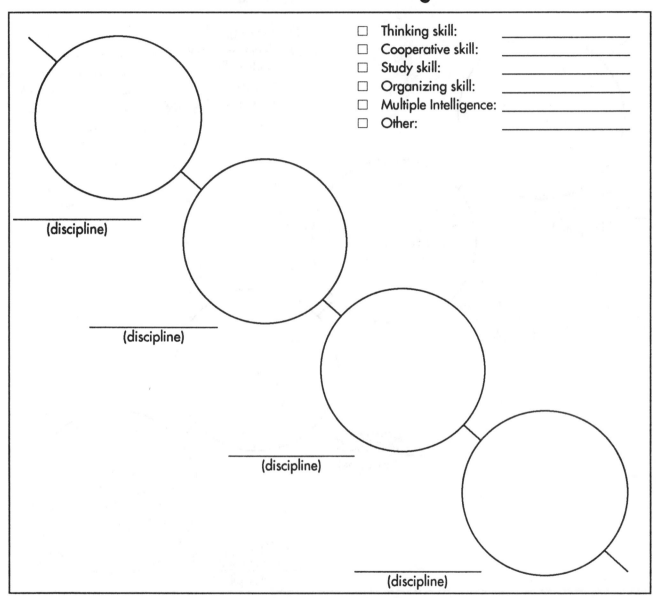

☐ Thinking skill: _____
☐ Cooperative skill: _____
☐ Study skill: _____
☐ Organizing skill: _____
☐ Multiple Intelligence: _____
☐ Other: _____

(discipline)

(discipline)

(discipline)

(discipline)

## Notes & Reflections

*Think ahead as team members plan their topics and units for next semester. Target several meta-skills to thread through the curricular content.*

# ▶ Think Ahead: Design ◀

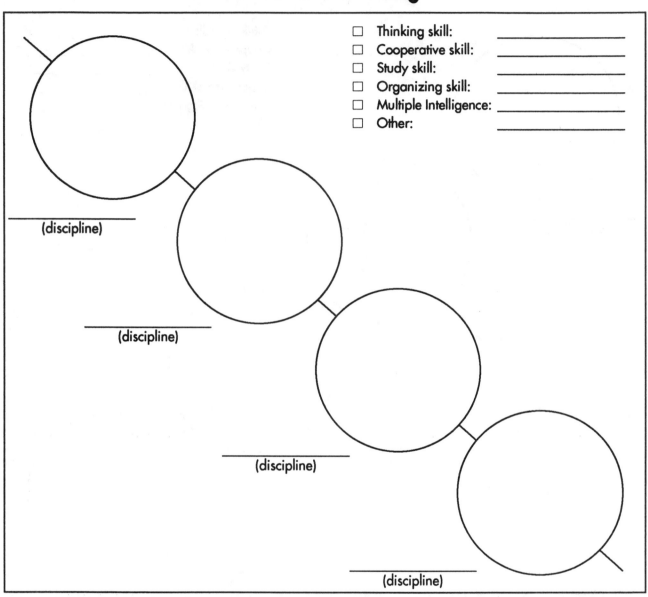

☐ Thinking skill: _____
☐ Cooperative skill: _____
☐ Study skill: _____
☐ Organizing skill: _____
☐ Multiple Intelligence: _____
☐ Other: _____

(discipline)

(discipline)

(discipline)

(discipline)

## Notes & Reflections

*Think again as team members outline additional units of study with appropriate meta-skills to thread through the subject matter content.*

# ► Think Again: Design ◄

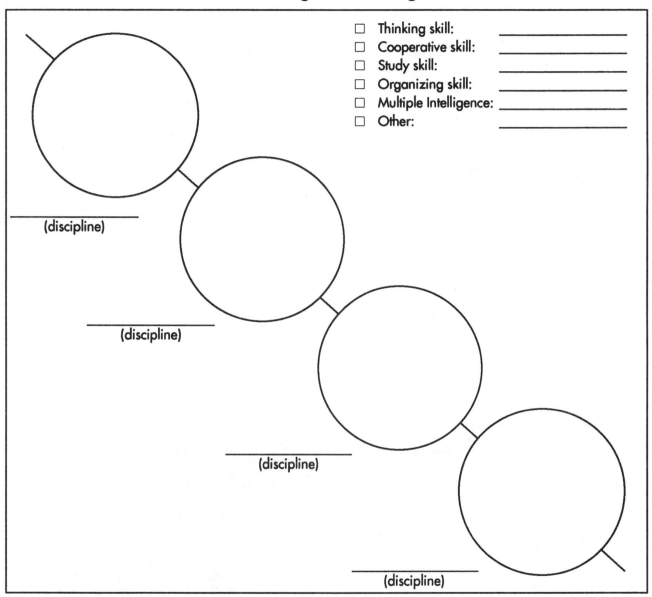

- ☐ Thinking skill: _____
- ☐ Cooperative skill: _____
- ☐ Study skill: _____
- ☐ Organizing skill: _____
- ☐ Multiple Intelligence: _____
- ☐ Other: _____

_____
(discipline)

_____
(discipline)

_____
(discipline)

_____
(discipline)

## Notes & Reflections

TO VIEW CURRICULA THROUGH A KALEIDOSCOPE IS TO REARRANGE PATTERNS AND DESIGNS.

# Model 8

# INTEGRATED

*This interdisciplinary approach matches subjects for overlaps in topics and concepts with some team teaching in an authentic integrated model.*

Kaleidoscope—new patterns
and designs that use the basic
elements of each discipline

*"I call a complete and generous education that which fits [an individual] to perform justly, skillfully, and magnanimously all the offices, both private and public, of peace and war."*
—John Milton

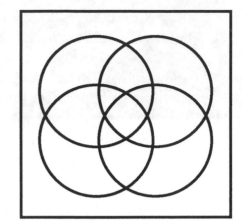

## What Is The Integrated Model?

The integrated curricular model represents a cross-disciplinary approach similar to the shared model. The integrated model blends the four major disciplines by setting curricular priorities in each and finding the overlapping skills, concepts, and attitudes in all four. As in the shared model, the integration is a result of sifting ideas out of subject matter content, not laying an idea over the subjects as in the webbed themes approach. The integration sprouts from within the various disciplines and matches are made among them as commonalities emerge.

## What Does It Look Like?

At the middle school or secondary school, an integrated curriculum is conceived as an interdisciplinary team struggles with an overloaded curriculum. As a team, they decide to "selectively abandon" pieces from the traditional curriculum. Armed with prudent priorities for the discipline, the four team members begin to explore overlapping priorities, concepts that undergird their very disciplines. One such overlap they discover early on is the concept of argument and evidence. It works well in Math, Science, Language Arts, and Social Studies. It's a first step.

EXAMPLE:

In Math, Science, Social Studies, Fine Arts, Language Arts, and Practical Arts, teachers look for patterning models and approach content through these patterns.

In the elementary classroom an integrated model that illustrates the critical elements of this approach is the whole language movement in which reading, writing, listening, and speaking skills spring from a wholistic, literature-based program that taps all the energies of the learner and the disciplines. Whole language is a philosophy of learning that embraces an integrated curriculum as opposed to the more traditional, fragmented model in which each subject is addressed separately and apart from the others. Integrated models such as whole language are designed with the learner as the focus, while fragmented models are designed with the content as the focal point.

## What Does It Sound Like?

"Unless we educate for wholeness in person and wholeness of our earth planet, we are not really intelligent. In our school subjects, we have an opportunity to study humankind as a family, and the heart as the body of that family. We have the possibility of developing a curriculum which is like a map of its dreams and its history, a map of interconnections. Interdisciplinary methods try to avoid squeezing the life out of one part and blowing it up in another."

—M.C. Richards

## What Are The Advantages?

A distinct advantage of the integrated model is the ease with which the learner is lead to the interconnectedness and interrelationships among the various disciplines. The integrated model builds understanding across departments and fosters appreciation of staff knowledge and expertise. The integrated model, when successfully implemented, approaches the ideal learning environment for an integrated day externally and for an integrated learner focus internally. The integrated model also carries with it an inherent motivational factor as students and ideas gain momentum from class to class.

## What Are The Disadvantages?

It is a difficult, sophisticated model to implement fully. This integrated model requires highly skilled staff, confident in the priority concepts, skills, and attitudes that pervade their respective disciplines. In addition, the integrated curriculum requires interdepartmental teams with blocks of planning and teaching time in common, which often means major restructuring of schedules. To integrate curricula with explicit attention to the genuine conceptual priorities of each discipline requires the commitment of a myriad of resources.

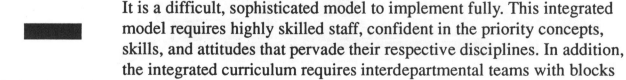

## When Is This Integrated Model Useful?

This integrated model is most appropriately used with a cross-departmental team of volunteers who are willing to commit time and energy to the integration process. It is helpful to start with a small pilot project such as a three- to four-week unit. Summer curriculum-writing time or designed-release time during the semester is most likely necessary to fully explore this model.

Once a pilot is in place, further team commitment can be made. But, a word of caution is needed here. It is not advisable for a school to adopt this model as a school-wide reform without first giving it serious thought. Remember, committed volunteers across departments are the critical elements for this complex model. Eventually, as team members work together learning about the other disciplines and the other team members, the units can be planned for longer periods of time. But this is a gradual process of building confidence and trust as team curriculum designers.

MEANWHILE, OVER THE SUMMER, MEETINGS AT THE MINDFUL SCHOOL ARE FREQUENT AND HEATED. SUE, TOM, MARIA, BOB, AND PRISCILLA ARE EXPLORING POSSIBILITIES AND <u>LOOKING FOR MATCH-UPS.</u>

I LIKED THE WEBBED MODEL WE TRIED LAST YEAR. BUT SOMETIMES, I FELT LIKE I WAS MANIPULATING AND CONTRIVING MY CONTENT A BIT. WHAT IF WE TRIED A FULL-BLOWN INTERDISCIPLINARY TEAM APPROACH THIS YEAR AND LOOKED FOR THE NATURAL OVERLAPS?

YES, I AGREE WITH YOU, SUE. BUT WHAT IF WE ONLY FIND A FEW GENUINE AREAS OF OVERLAP? HOW DO WE COME TO TERMS WITH THAT WITHOUT ARTIFICIALLY STRETCHING OUR TRUE PRIORITIES? LET'S TRY THE INTEGRATED APPROACH IN A PILOT ONLY. MAYBE PLAN A THREE-WEEK SEGMENT...

GEE, THAT'S AN EXCITING IDEA! I LIKE COMING FROM THE HEART OF EACH DISCIPLINE AND THEN LOOKING FOR THE OVERLAPPING CONCEPTS. LET'S GO FOR IT!

I THINK I KNOW WHAT YOU MEAN, TOM. WE SHOULD FIRST LOOK AT OUR INDIVIDUAL CONTENT PRIORITIES AND THEN SIFT OUT CONCEPTS, IDEAS, AND ATTITUDES THAT HAVE OVERLAPPING ELEMENTS. FOR EXAMPLE, IN MY DNA UNIT, ASIDE FROM THE TECHNICAL INFORMATION ABOUT GENETIC ENGINEERING THERE ARE MORAL AND ETHICAL ISSUES. THOSE ISSUES MIGHT OVERLAP WITH SOCIAL STUDIES AND LANGUAGE ARTS. THERE ARE ALSO A NUMBER OF MATHEMATICAL CONCEPTS INHERENT IN THE DNA MODEL.

*An interdisciplinary or grade-level team brings their conceptual priorities together, looking for overlaps in concepts, skills, and attitudes as well as content concepts.*

# ► Samples ◄

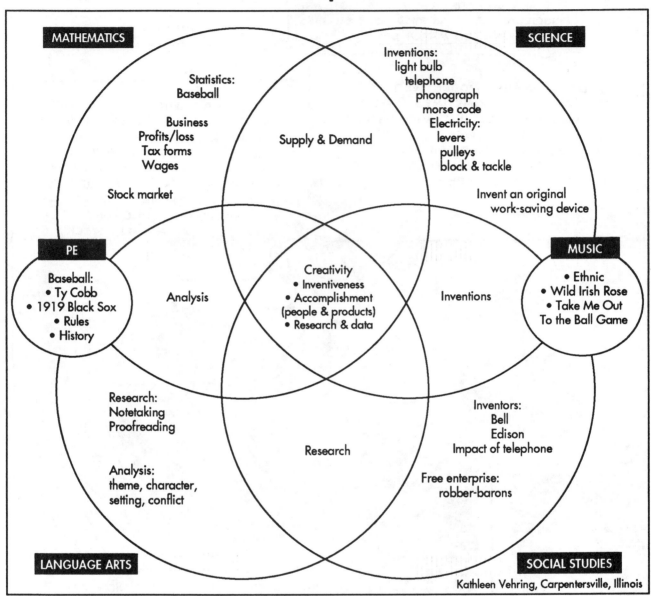

**MATHEMATICS**

Statistics:
Baseball

Business
Profits/loss
Tax forms
Wages

Stock market

Supply & Demand

**SCIENCE**

Inventions:
light bulb
telephone
phonograph
morse code
Electricity:
levers
pulleys
block & tackle

Invent an original
work-saving device

**PE**

Baseball:
• Ty Cobb
• 1919 Black Sox
• Rules
• History

Analysis

Creativity
• Inventiveness
• Accomplishment
(people & products)
• Research & data

Inventions

**MUSIC**

• Ethnic
• Wild Irish Rose
• Take Me Out
To the Ball Game

Research:
Notetaking
Proofreading

Analysis:
theme, character,
setting, conflict

Research

Inventors:
Bell
Edison
Impact of telephone

Free enterprise:
robber-barons

**LANGUAGE ARTS**

**SOCIAL STUDIES**

Kathleen Vehring, Carpentersville, Illinois

## Notes & Reflections

Using their content priorities, team members look beyond the topics to the concepts, skills, and attitudes they target in their separate disciplines. Armed with these basics, the team looks for the overlapping ideas that emerge as common ground among the four disciplines. The similarities emerge from the content pieces.

*Think back to units just finished. As an interdisciplinary or grade-level team lists topics and units, the concepts are sifted out. Finally, with these concepts or priorities, the basic curriculum content carries the overlapping ideas.*

# ► Think Back: Re-Design ◄

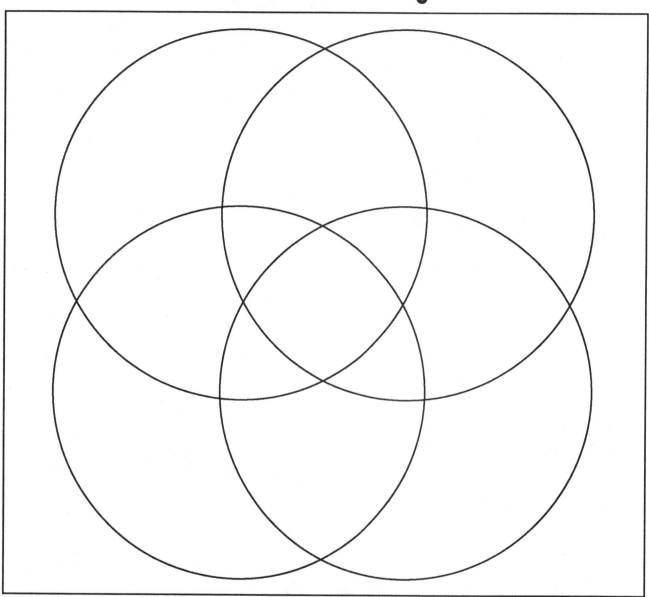

## Notes & Reflections

*Think ahead to units coming up. Try to list content, sort out concepts, and look for overlaps that create new arrangements that integrate ideas.*

## ▶ Think Ahead: Design ◀

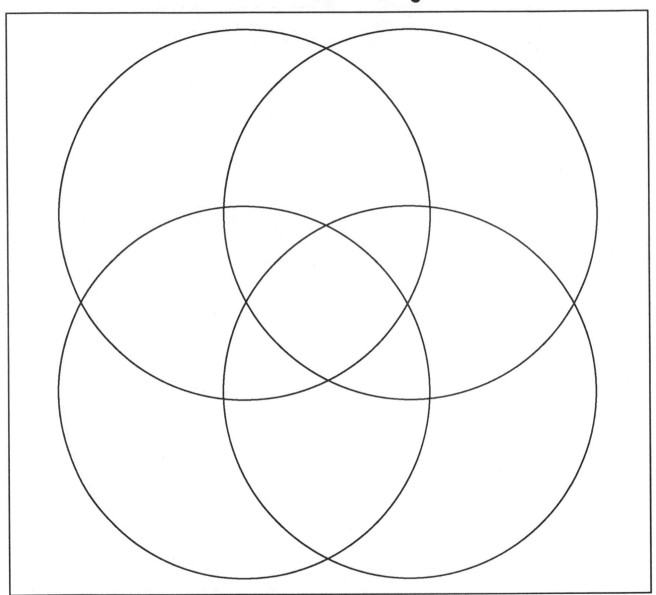

## Notes & Reflections

*Think again. Plan with a team using content, concepts, and overlapping ideas to integrate the various curricula.*

# ▶ Think Again:  Design ◀

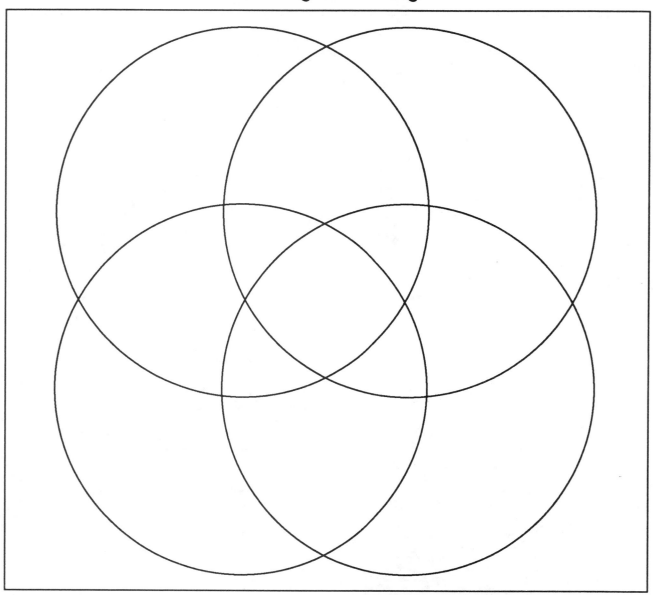

## Notes & Reflections

IT'S AN UP-CLOSE AND PERSONAL VIEW THROUGH THE MICROSCOPE.

# Model **9**

---

# IMMERSED

---

*The disciplines become part of the learner's lens of expertise; the learner filters all content through this lens and becomes immersed in his or her own experience.*

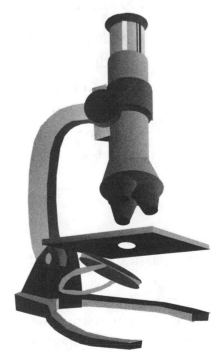

Microscope—intensely personal view that allows microscopic explanation as all content is filtered through lens of interest and expertise

*"The one real object of education is to have a [person] in the condition of continually asking questions."*—Bishop Mondell Creighton

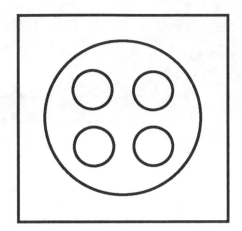

## What Is The Immersed Model?

Afficionados, graduate students, doctoral candidates, and post-doctoral fellows are totally immersed in a field of study. They filter all curricular content learning through one microscopic lens. This individual integrates all data, from every field and discipline, by funneling the ideas through his or her area of intense interest. In this model of integrated curricula, the integration is internally and intrinsically accomplished by the learner with little or no extrinsic or outside intervention.

## What Does It Look Like?

At the secondary or university level, the doctoral candidate is immersed in biochemistry. Her area of specialization is chemical bonding of substances. Even though her field is chemistry, she devours the software programs in *computer science* classes so she can analyze her data in simulated lab experiments, saving days of tedious lab work. She accepts an offer to learn *patent law* in order to protect her ideas for her company and to protect her company from liability cases. All learning paths are sparked by her passion for her field.

Likewise, a six-year-old first-grader writes incessantly about butterflies, bugs, spiders, insects, and creepy crawlies of all sorts. Her art work is modeled on the symmetrical design of ladybugs and the patterns of butterflies. She counts and mounts, frames and sings about

EXAMPLE:

**Student or doctoral candidate has an area of expert interest and sees all learning through that lens.**

them. Her interest in insect biology is already consuming her. The books she chooses reflect her internal integration of her interest in learning of her subject.

## What Does It Sound Like?

An immersed learner might say something like this: "I'm totally immersed in my work. It is a labor of love and my laboratory is my life. It seems that everything I *choose* to pursue with any fervor is directly related to my intellectual interest." Just as the writer records notes or the artist makes sketches, the immersed learner is constantly making connections to his subject. With this self-directed, self-initiating learner, the teacher's mission often becomes one of getting out of the learner's way.

## What Are The Advantages?

Of course, the ultimate advantage is that integration must take place within the learner, which is exactly what is illustrated in this model. The learner is self-driven by an insatiable hunger to understand. "The more we know, the more we know we don't know" becomes an unhidden truth. As the student digs deeper into a field of interest, the related areas and new pathways seem unending. Actually, the immersed learner exhibits phenomenal discipline as he or she develops this intense focus. Of course, another plus is that the connection-making of this learner is often made *explicit* to other learners as the expert makes advances in the field.

## What Are The Disadvantages?

The filtering of all ideas through a single microscopic lens may occur too prematurely or in too narrow a focus. Richness of experience and broad bases from which to review a specialization bring depth and dimension to the learner's perspective. A liberal background that crosscuts the major disciplines provides the most fertile ground for enriching this learner's experience. The more varied, in fact, the better, at least early in the educational process. There is plenty of time to specialize later.

ALL LEARNING—MATH, SCIENCE, HISTORY—IS FILTERED THROUGH THE LEARNER'S LENS OF EXPERIENCE AND EXPERTISE.

## When Is This Immersed Model Useful?

This model is not prescribed through a deliberate plan. The immersed model of integration seems to just happen. One cannot engineer the internal integration. It resides solely within the learner. However, once this form of integration is noted, the teaching team can certainly facilitate the fusion process with calculated synthesis. Broad, varied content, unified with overriding skills, concepts, and attitudes work well with this immersed learner who automatically sees lots of connections.

A GRADUATE OF THE MINDFUL SCHOOL SYSTEM, AND THE UNIVERSITY, TELLS HIS COLLEAGUE...

I'D BEEN WITH THE FIRM FOR FIVE YEARS AS A CHEMICAL RESEARCHER AND LIKED TO JUST STICK TO THE LABORATORY. BUT THEN I HAD TO LEARN THE CAD/CAM PROGRAMS TO USE THE TECHNICAL EQUIPMENT. THE TIME I SAVED BY USING THE COMPUTER SIMULATIONS WAS UNBELIEVABLE. THEN I STARTED SPENDING A LOT MORE TIME ON THE PATENTING PROCESS AND STARTED LOOKING AT PATENT LAW. NOW THE COMPANY WANTS ME TO GO TO LAW SCHOOL.

NOT ONLY THAT, IN ORDER TO DEAL WITH OUR JAPANESE MANUFACTURERS, I'VE STARTED STUDYING JAPANESE! I NEED TO HAVE SOME UNDERSTANDING OF THE LANGUAGE—AT LEAST I'D LIKE TO BE ABLE TO UNDERSTAND SOME OF WHAT I HEAR. THE LEARNING NEVER STOPS. WHO KNOWS WHAT I'LL GET INTO NEXT!

*The immersed learner reads and learns through his or her area of interest and reflects this in both input and output modes.*

## ► Samples ◄

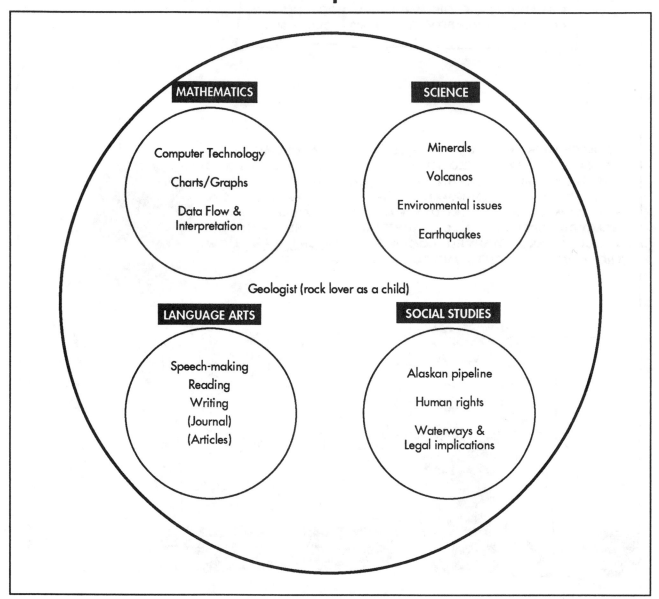

**MATHEMATICS**

Computer Technology

Charts/Graphs

Data Flow &
Interpretation

**SCIENCE**

Minerals

Volcanos

Environmental issues

Earthquakes

Geologist (rock lover as a child)

**LANGUAGE ARTS**

Speech-making
Reading
Writing
(Journal)
(Articles)

**SOCIAL STUDIES**

Alaskan pipeline

Human rights

Waterways &
Legal implications

## Notes & Reflections

The immersed learner funnels most learning through his or her area of interest. This learner uses a refined selection process that automatically screens input and seeks out the areas that have explicit and/or implicit connections. The more expert the expert is the more fine-tuned the selection process is.

*In an individual effort, use your own personal interest area and jot down related topics in each of the four disciplines.*

# ► **Think Back: Re-Design** ◄

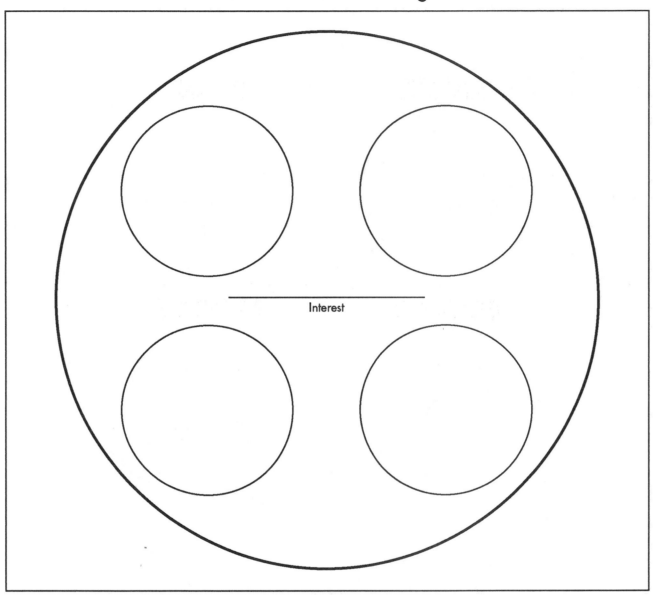

Interest

## Notes & Reflections

*Now, working alone, think of an emerging interest and jot down related ideas in each of the four disciplines that you might want to explore.*

## ▶ Think Ahead: Design ◀

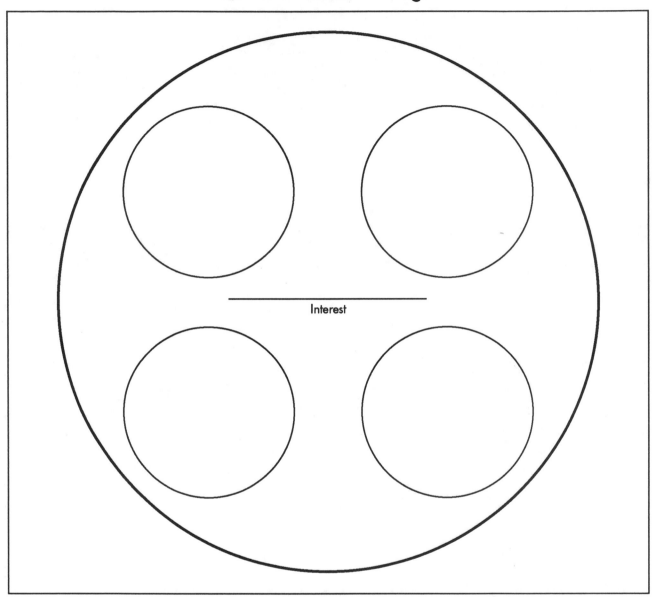

Interest

## Notes & Reflections

*On your own, think of another emerging interest. Try to relate topics from each discipline that are candidates for exploration.*

## ▶ Think Again: Design ◀

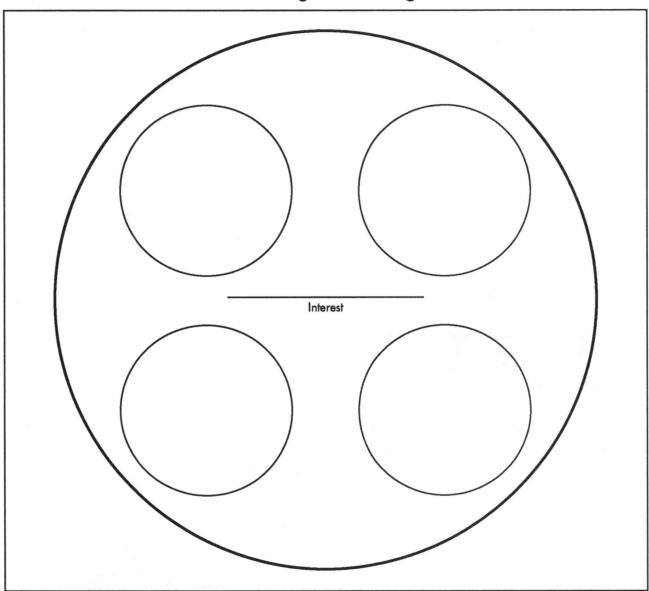

Interest

## Notes & Reflections

LEARNERS NETWORK WITH OTHERS BOTH WITHIN THEIR CHOSEN FIELD AND <u>OUTSIDE</u> THAT FIELD AS THEY CONTINUALLY LINK NEW IDEAS TO OLD.

# Model 10

## NETWORKED

*Learner filters all learning through the expert's eye and makes internal connections that lead to external networks of experts in related fields.*

Prism—a view that creates
multiple dimensions and
directions of focus

*"The education of a man is never completed until he dies."*—Robert E. Lee

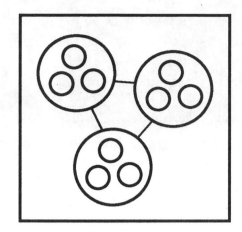

## What Is The Networked Model?

The networked model of integrated learning is an ongoing external source of input, forever providing new, extended, and extrapolated or refined ideas. The learner's professional network usually grows in obvious, and sometimes not so obvious, directions. In the search for knowledge, learners come to depend on this network as a primary source of information that they must filter through their own lens of expertise and interest.

In the networked model of integration, unlike in the earlier models, the learner directs the integration process through self-selection of the needed networks. Only the learners themselves, knowing the intricacies and dimensions of their field, can target the necessary resources. This model, like the others, develops and grows over time as needs propel the learner in new directions.

## What Does It Look Like?

This model of networked integration is seen to a limited extent in the elementary schools. Imagine a fifth grader who has had a keen interest in Indians since his toddler days of playing cowboys and Indians. His passion for Indian lore leads him into historical readings—

EXAMPLE:

**Architect, while adapting the CAD/CAM technology for design, networks with technical programmers and expands her knowledge base, just as she had traditionally done with interior designers.**

both fictional and non-fictional. His family, well aware of his intrigue with the Indians, hears about an archeological dig that recruits youngsters to actually participate in the dig as part of a summer program offered by a local college. As a result of this summer "camp," this learner meets people in a number of fields: an anthropologist, geologist, archeologist, and an illustrator, student of the fine arts, hired to represent the dig in drawings. This learner's networks are already taking shape. His natural interest has led him to others in the field who offer various levels of knowledge and insight that extend his learning.

## What Does It Sound Like?

The networked model sounds like a three- or four-way conference call that provides various avenues of exploration and explanation. Although these diverse ideas may not come all at once, the networked learner is open to multiple modes of input as divergent components are sifted and sorted to suit the need. This model sounds like network news pulling in pictures and stories from around the globe. The network is much like a satellite beaming signals here and there and receiving signals from everywhere.

## What Are The Advantages?

The advantages of the networked model are many. This integrated learning approach is extremely pro-active in nature, with the learner self-initiating the searches and following the newly emerging paths. The learner is stimulated with relevant information, skill, or concepts that move his learning along. The pluses of this model however, cannot be imposed on the learner, but rather must emerge from within. However, mentors can and do provide the necessary models to support this sophisticated stage of learning.

## What Are The Disadvantages?

The minuses of the networked model are familiar to those who have developed many diverse interests in their labor of love. It is easy to get side-tracked into one of the side ideas. It's also possible to get in over your head. A particular path seems inviting and useful, but suddenly becomes overwhelming. The benefits no longer outweigh the price one has to pay. Another drawback is that the networked model, if taken to extremes, can spread interests too thin and dilute a concentrated effort.

## When Is This Networked Model Useful?

This model, like the immersed model, often moves the onus of integration to the learner rather than to an outside instructional designer. However, it is an appropriate model to present to motivated learners. Tutors or mentors often suggest networking to extend the learner's horizons or provide a needed perspective. As networks evolve, serendipitous connections appear along the way. Often, these accidental findings propel the learner into new depths in the field or actually lead to the creation of a more specialized field. One such example in this modern day, of course, is the field of genetics, which has developed an area known as genetic engineering. This unfolding of a field is really the result of immersed expert learners networking with other immersed expert learners.

*Armed with a "mission in mind," the learner networks with two other experts in order to execute the "pet project."*

# ► Samples ◄

Learner's Mission: To survey for nutritional misconceptions and rewrite health curriculum to reflect modern concepts of nutrition.

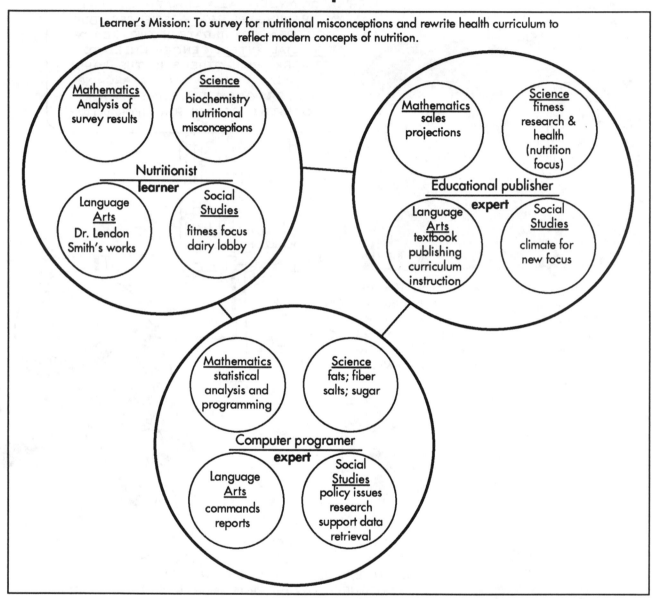

## Notes & Reflections

The learner is propelled by his/her area of interest to search out experts both inside and outside the field in order to extend and enrich the field.

*Think back to a pet project you once did. Track two "experts" you networked with in order to accomplish your task. Try to imagine how they pulled in all four disciplines to the expertise.*

# ▶ Think Back: Re-Design ◀

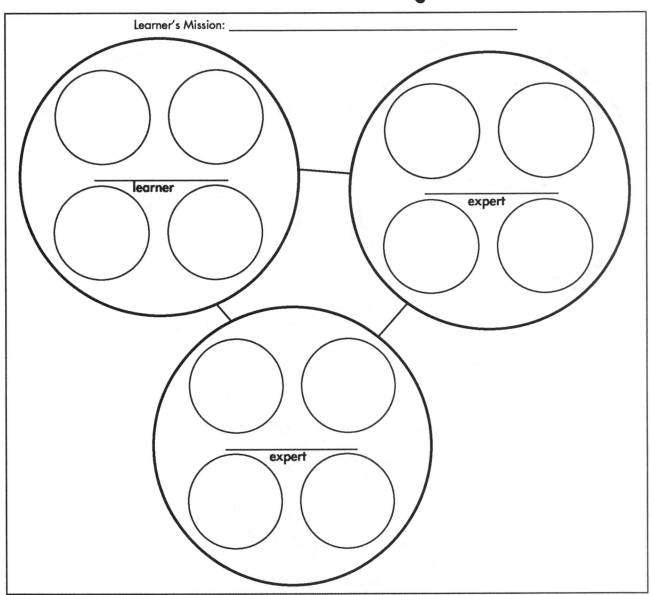

Learner's Mission: _____

learner

expert

expert

## Notes & Reflections

*Think ahead to a "pet project" you want to begin. Sketch out a scenario in which you will network with other experts. Try to imagine how they will use all four disciplines within their expertise.*

## ▶ Think Ahead: Design ◀

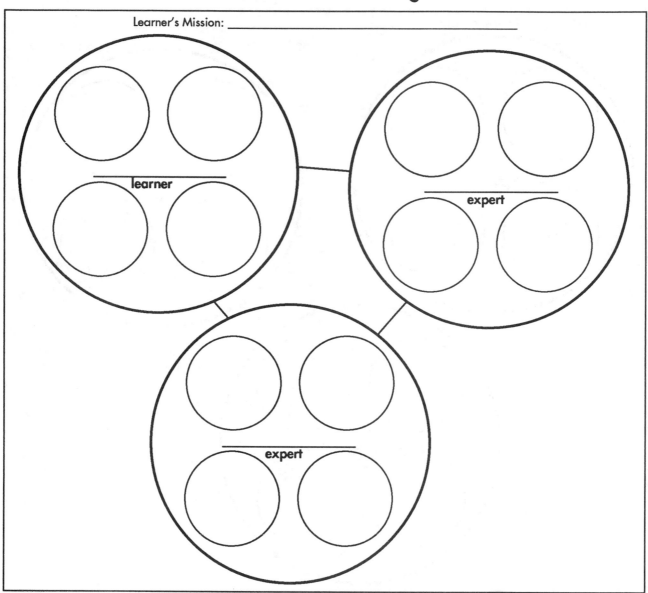

Learner's Mission: _____

learner

expert

expert

## Notes & Reflections

*Think again about a long-range "mission" and network to two experts who can help you execute your idea. Try to show how the four disciplines relate to each expert.*

# ▶ Think Again: Design ◀

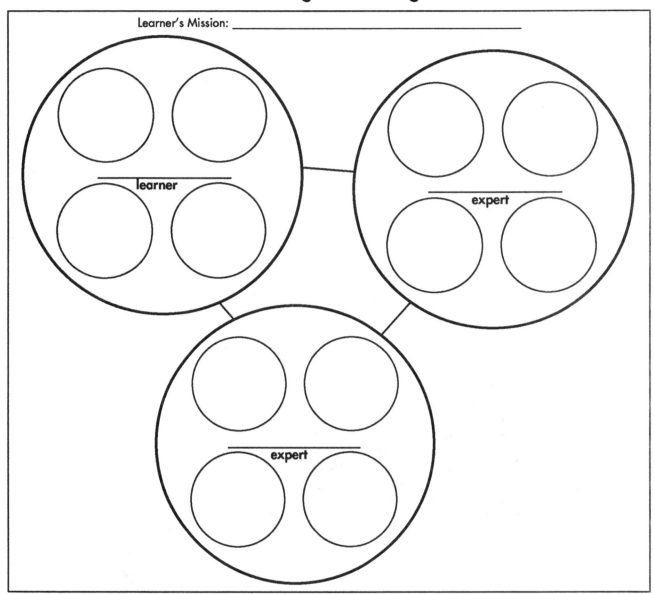

Learner's Mission: _____

## Notes & Reflections

THE TEN MODELS FOR INTEGRATED
LEARNING ARE JUST THE FIRST
STEPS TOWARD MAKING CONNECTIONS
FOR LESSONS AND LEARNERS. THESE
REFERENCES PROVIDE FURTHER
INSIGHTS TO HELP YOU CREATE
DESIGNS OF YOUR OWN.

# REFERENCES

Barell, J., *Teaching For Thoughtfulness*. Longman, New York and London, 1991.

Bellanca, J., *The Cooperative Think Tank*. Skylight Publishing, Palatine, Illinois, 1991.

Bellanca, J. and Fogarty, R., *Blueprints for Thinking in the Cooperative Classroom,* (Second Edition). Skylight Publishing, Palatine, Illinois, 1991.

Beyer, B., *Practical Strategies for the Teaching of Thinking*. Allyn and Bacon, Boston, 1987.

Bloom, A., *The Closing of the American Mind.* Simon and Schuster, New York, 1987.

Bloom, B.S., editor, *Taxonomy of Educational Objectives: The Classification of Educational Goals, Handbook I: Cognitive Domain*. Longman, New York, 1984.

Brandt, R., "On Teaching Thinking: A Conversation with Arthur Costa" in *Educational Leadership*. Vol. 45, No. 7, April, 1988.

Bruner, J., *Toward a Theory of Instruction*. Belknap Press, Cambridge, Massachusetts, 1975.

Carbol, Barry, Project Leader, *The Intermediate Program: Learning in British Columbia*. Ministry of Education, Educational Programs, Victoria, Province of British Columbia, 1990.

"Cogitare, Newsletter of the ASCD Network on Teaching Thinking: Integrating Curriculum." Vol. 5, Issue 2, Skylight Publishing, Palatine, Illinois, 1991.

Costa, A. L., *On Teaching For Intelligent Behavior*. Skylight Publishing, Palatine, Illinois (in press).

Costa, A. L., "What Human Beings Do When They Behave Intelligently and How They Can Become More So" in *Developing Minds: A Resource Book for Teaching Thinking, Vol. 1*. Association for Supervision and Curriculum Development, Alexandria, Virginia, 1991.

Costa, A. L. and Garmston, R., "The Art of Cognitive Coaching: Supervision for Intelligent Teaching." Paper presented at the Annual Conference of the Association for Supervision and Curriculum Development, Chicago, 1988.

Eisner, E., "What Really Counts in Schools" in *Educational Leadership*. Vol. 48, No. 5, February, 1991.

Elvin, L., *The Place of Common Sense in Educational Thought*. Unwin Educational Books, London, 1977.

Emerson, R.W., *Selected Essays*. Penguin, New York, 1982.

Feurstein, R., *Instrumental Enrichment*. University Park Press, Baltimore, 1980.

Fogarty, R., *Designs for Cooperative Interactions*. Skylight Publishing, Palatine, Illinois, 1990.

Fogarty, R., "From Training to Transfer: The Role of Creativity in the Adult Learner." Doctoral Dissertation, University of Chicago, Loyola, Illinois, 1989.

Fogarty, R. and Bellanca, J., *Patterns for Thinking, Patterns for Transfer*. Skylight Publishing, Palatine, Illinois, 1989.

Fogarty, R. and Bellanca, J., *Teach Them Thinking*. Skylight Publishing, Palatine, Illinois, 1986.

Fullan, M., *The Meaning of Educational Change*. Teachers College Press, New York, 1982.

Hirsch, E. D., Jr., *Cultural Literacy*. Hougton-Mifflin, Boston, 1987.

Hirst, P. H., *Knowledge and Curriculum*. Routledge and Kegan Paul, London, 1964.

Hirst, P. H. and Peters, R. S., "The Curriculum" in *Conflicting Conceptions of Curriculum*, edited by E. Eisner and E. Vallance. McCutchen, Berkeley, California, 1974.

Hord, S. and Loucks, S., *A Concerns-based Model for Delivery of Inservice*. CBAM Project, Research and Development Center for Teacher Education, The University of Texas at Austin, Austin, Texas, 1980.

Howard, Dara Lee, "From Need To Knowledge: Solving Information Problems." Doctoral Dissertation, University of Hawaii, Honolulu, (in progress).

Hunter, M., *Teach for Transfer*. TIP Publications, El Segundo, California, 1971.

Hyde, A. and Bizar, M., *Thinking in Context*. Longman, White Plains, New York, 1989.

Jacobs, H. H., Interdisciplinary Curriculum: Design and Implementation. ASCD, Alexandria, Virginia, 1990.

Jacobs, H. H. and Borland, J. H., "The Interdisciplinary Concept Model: Theory and Practice" in *Gifted Child Quarterly*. Fall, 1986.

Jones, B. F.; Palinescor, A.; Ogle, D. S.; and Carr, E. G., *Strategic Teaching and Learning: Cognitive Instruction in the Content Areas*. Association for Supervision and Curriculum Development, Alexandria, Virginia, 1987.

Jones, B. F.; Tinzmann, M.; Friedman, L.; and Walker, B., *Teaching Thinking Skills: English/Language Arts*. National Educational Association, Washington, D.C., 1987.

Joyce, B. R., *Improving America's Schools*. Longman, White Plains, New York, 1986.

Joyce, B. R. and Showers, B., "Improving Inservice Training: The Message of Research" in *Educational Leadership*. Vol. 43:8, February, 1990.

Joyce, B. R. and Showers, B., *Power and Staff Development Through Research and Training*. ASCD, Alexandria, Virginia, 1983.

Lawton, D., *Class, Culture and Curriculum*. Routledge and Kegan Paul, Boston, 1975.

Lazear, D., *Seven Ways of Knowing*. Skylight Publishing, Palatine, Illinois, 1991.

Lazear, D., *Seven Ways of Teaching*. Skylight Publishing, Palatine, Illinois, (in press).

Marcus, S., "Are Four Food Groups Enough?" Doctoral Dissertation, Walden University, Minneapolis, Minnesota, (expected February, 1992).

Marzano, R. J. and Arredondo, D. E.,"Restructuring Schools Through the Teaching of Thinking Skills" in *Educational Leadership*. Vol. 43:8, May, 1986.

Marzano, R. J.; Pickering, D.; and Brandt, R.,"Integrating Instruction Programs Through Dimensions of Learning" in *Educational Leadership*. Vol. 47:5, 1990.

Meeth, L. R., "Interdisciplinary Studies: Integration of Knowledge and Experience" in *Change*. Vol. 10:6-9, 1978.

Osborn, A. F., *Applied Imagination*. Scribner, New York, 1963.

Parnes, S. J., *Aha! Insights Into Creative Behavior*. D.O.K. Publishing, Buffalo, New York, 1975.

Perkins, D. N., *Knowledge As Design*. Lawrence Erlbaum Associates, Hillsdale, New Jersey, 1986.

Perkins, D. N., *Schools of Thought: The Necessary Shape of Education*. Boston, 1991.

Perkins, D. N., "Thinking Frames," paper delivered at ASCD Conference on Approaches to Teaching Thinking, Alexandria, Virginia, 1988.

Perkins, D. N. and Salomon, G., "Are Cognitive Skills Content Bound?" in *Educational Leadership*. January - February, 1989.

Perkins, D. N. and Salomon, G., "Teaching For Transfer" in *Educational Leadership*. Vol. 46:1, September, 1988.

Piaget, J., *The Epistemology of Interdisciplinary Relationships*. Organization for Economic Cooperation and Development, Paris, 1972.

Posner, M. I. and Keele, S. W., "Skill Learning" in *Second Handbook of Research on Teaching*, R. M. W. Travers, editor. Rand McNally, Chicago, 1973.

Ravitch, D., "Why Educators Resist a Basic Required Curriculum" in *The Great School Debate*, edited by B. Gross and R. Gross. Simon and Schuster, New York, 1985.

Ravitch, D. and Finn, C., "The Humanities: A Truly Challenging Course of Study" in *The Great School Debate*, edited by B. Gross and R. Gross. Simon and Schuster, New York, 1985.

Resnick, L. B. and Klopfer, L., *Toward the Thinking Curriculum: Current Cognitive Research, 1989 ASCD Yearbook*. Association for Supervision and Curriculum Development, Washington, D.C., 1989.

Richards, M. C., *The Public School and the Education of the Whole Person*. The Pilgrim Press, Philadelphia and New York, 1980.

Sergiovanni, T., "Will We Ever Have A True Profession?" in *Educational Leadership*. Vol. 44:8, May, 1987.

Sternberg, R. J., "How Can We Teach Intelligence?" in *Educational Leadership*. Vol. 42:1, September, 1984.

Sternberg, R. J., *Intelligence Applied. Understanding and Increasing Your Intellectual Skills*. Harcourt Brace Jovanovich, Boston, 1986.

Tyler, R. W., "The Five Most Significant Curriculum Events in the Twentieth Century" in *Educational Leadership*. Vol. 44:4, December 1986 - January 1987.

Vars, G. F., *Interdisciplinary Teaching in the Middle Grades*. National Middle School Association, Columbus, Ohio, 1987.

Wittrock, M. C., "Replacement and Nonreplacement Strategies in Children's Problem Solving" in *Journal of Educational Psychology*. Vol. 58:2, 1967.

# Additional resources to increase your teaching expertise...

**SKYLIGHT PUBLISHING, INC.**

**1**

## *The Skylight Catalog*

The Skylight Catalog presents a selection of the best publications from nationally recognized authorities on **cooperative learning, thinking, whole language, self-esteem, substance abuse prevention, multiple intelligences** and **school restructuring**.

*The* **IRI** *Group*

**2**

## *Training*

IRI training is available through inservices, seminars and conferences. Gain practical techniques and strategies for implementing the latest findings from educational research. IRI training provides necessary educational skills at a cost educators can afford.

*The* **IRI** *Group*

**3**

## *Training of Trainers*

IRI provides inservice training for experienced educators who are designated to train other staff members. The training for trainers provides techniques for effectively introducing the latest strategies to peer educators.

### To receive a free copy of the Skylight Catalog, or for more information about trainings offered by IRI, contact:

**IRI/Skylight Publishing, Inc.**
200 E. Wood Street, Suite 250, Palatine, Illinois 60067
800-922-4474 (In Illinois 708-991-6300)
FAX 708-991-6420

There are

one-story intellects,

two-story intellects, and three-story

intellects with skylights. All fact collectors who have

no aim beyond their facts are one-story men. Two-story men compare,

reason, generalize, using the labor of fact collectors as their own.

Three-story men idealize, imagine, predict—

their best illumination comes

from above the skylight.

—*Oliver Wendell*

*Holmes*

**SKYLIGHT
PUBLISHING, INC.**